PELICAN BOOKS
A122
BALLET
ARNOLD L. HASKELL

BALLET

A Complete Guide to Appreciation: History, Aesthetics, Ballets, Dancers

ARNOLD L. HASKELL

PENGUIN BOOKS

Penguin Books Ltd, Harmondsworth, Middlesex

U.S.A.: Penguin Books Inc., 3300 Clipper Mill Road, Baltimore 11, Md
[*Educational Representative:*
D. C. Heath & Co., 285 Columbus Avenue, Boston 16, Mass]

CANADA: Penguin Books (Canada) Ltd, 47 Green Street,
Saint Lambert, Montreal, P.Q.

AUSTRALIA: Penguin Books Pty Ltd, 762 Whitehorse Road,
Mitcham, Victoria

SOUTH AFRICA: Penguin Books (S.A.) Pty Ltd, Gibraltar House
Regents Road, Sea Point, Cape Town

—

First published July 1938
Reprinted 1938 (twice), 1940, 1943
Revised edition 1945
Reprinted 1945
Revised editions 1949, 1951, 1955

Made and printed in Great Britain
by Hazell Watson and Viney Ltd
Aylesbury and London

Contents

List of Illustrations

List of Illustrations

ACKNOWLEDGEMENTS

The photographs reproduced in the inset are from the following sources: Walter E. Owen (Plate 2); Maurice Seymour (Plates 3 and 10); Anthony (Plates 6, 7, 8, 16, and 23); Photo Lido (Plate 9); Photo-Lipnitzki (Plate 12); Duncan Melvin (Plate 13); G. B. L. Wilson (Plates 17, 18, 19, 20a, 20b, 22, and 24); Jacques Mairesse (Plate 21). The remainder of the plates have been made from photographs lent by the author.

Preface to New Edition, 1955

BALLET first appeared as a Pelican book in July 1938, since when there have been a number of revised editions.

So great have been the changes in the ballet scene between 1938 and 1953, and especially during the last few years, that a partial revision is no longer possible. The main changes must be embodied in the text itself and no longer tacked on, and the book must be recast in such a way as to make it a guide to contemporary ballet for a long time to come.

In 1938 the attention of a limited though growing public was focused on *ballet russe*. Our young company at Sadler's Wells was developing splendidly, and connoisseurs talked of *The Rake's Progress* and of a certain promising Margot Fonteyn, but it was still very much a local affair. We had seen nothing of Balanchine's work in the United States, or of the results of Lifar's reviving influence on the old French tradition as shown by Roland Petit. The Ballet meant Russian (*émigré*) ballet, and any other brand needed considerable explanation and a certain amount of apology. *Les snobs* would not touch it at any price.

To-day there is far too much ballet and too few ideas; there are too many little girls wishing to become dancers and too few boys.

Ballet is an art of tradition, and the chapters on the history and aesthetics of the art must therefore remain unchanged; they are true whatever developments may take place. The main changes are in the contemporary scene and in the examples I have chosen for a practical application of the chapter on the aesthetics of ballet. I have tried, as far as possible, to avoid using as examples young dancers with their careers ahead of them or ballets that have no permanent value, other-

9

wise this new volume might be out of date before publication.

Things have speeded up since 1938; companies are formed and go into liquidation in a matter of months.

Once again I must thank my old friend Allen Lane for suggesting the writing of this book at a time when its success was so far from obvious.

ARNOLD L. HASKELL

34 Walton Street, London SW3
1955

Lifar says there oughth't to be any music.
Just noises.

THE LUNATIC FRINGE

CHAPTER ONE

Introductory

The present-day popularity of ballet – Strong influence of the audience – The ignorance of the young dancer – The importance of ballet as an artistic medium – The scheme of the book

BEFORE the war ballet was seasonal, a luxury that appealed to a restricted public. To-day in London there is ballet throughout the year. In the summer months of 1953 within a period of six weeks six companies performed, all of them with box-office success. The film studios have woken up to the fact of ballet's popularity, and have not only given us a series of shocking ballet films but have raided the ballet for stars which with few exceptions they have misused. This in its turn has increased the public until the art is in danger from its very popularity. And popularity constitutes a very real danger when it leads to the lowering of standards, as it did once before after the great days of romanticism. Then ballet found its way into the music-hall, neglected by serious painters and composers, a mere incident in an evening of light entertainment.

Gone indeed are the many jokes about the anaemic-looking, long-haired youths, and the short-haired, untidy women in hand-spun fabrics who enthused or muttered the current formula of 'What fun, how amusing, my dear'. Ballet still has its small lunatic band of hangers-on who make themselves conspicuous both sartorially and vocally,[1] but it has gained a great new public. The man in the street has discovered it and is so enchanted with his discovery that the ballet has become habit. He has found out that though the repertory of works is strictly limited, the performances themselves vary enormously,

1. See Glossary, under *Balletomane*, and illustration, page 10.

and he begins to find a keen pleasure in comparing the various sylphs he has seen during the past year. Before he knows where he is, he has become a critic.

It is possible to be carried away by the beauty of ballet, one of the very last strongholds of theatrical illusion, without possessing any critical standards or any backgrounds of knowledge, but only the trained eye will reap the maximum of pleasure from a performance – the man who is conscious not merely of his enjoyment, but of the reasons behind it.

There are two parties to every theatrical manifestation: the performers and their public; and it is ultimately the public who dictate the quality of the performance. The hypercritical public of the Imperial Russian theatres, those old *habitués* who could count every beat and who could in imagination dance every movement, were responsible for the triumph of a Pavlova.

It was Pavlova who once told the present writer: 'The public here is so exceedingly generous that while it warms my heart it does not help me. To-night, I know that I did not dance the *Dying Swan* as well as usual, but the applause was exactly the same. I would have been pleased if it had been just a little less.' Only because she was hypercritical of herself did Pavlova maintain her high standard, and she had learned to be hypercritical from her first audiences in Russia, and from the highly evolved system of training that formed her.

To-day we are living in an age of rapid results. There is no reason to believe that our dancers have less artistic talent than those of the past, and without any doubt the quantity of their technique has grown. But to-day the dancer shows herself after a shorter period of training and dances far more, in roles that vary from romantic classicism to acrobatics. Neither the dancer nor the company have the time to study or to rest. More than ever, therefore, the dancer depends upon the critical standards of the audience. But the audience, recruited

perhaps from a viewing of *The Red Shoes*, has formed its
critical standards from the young dancers, and is prepared to
applaud on the slightest provocation.

*The need of the dancers and their audience is identical; a back-
ground of knowledge that will develop the critical faculties.*

I have tried in this book to prepare such a background, both
for the spectator and for the young dancer. No art can be
learnt from a book, but a book can help the tyro to sort out
his own loose impressions, and to form for himself a basis of
criticism that will add, not only to his pleasure, but, in the end,
to the healthy development of the art.

Ballet is essentially an art of tradition, a tradition that is a
living force. Music has its score, the drama its book, and the
paintings of the past can be seen on the walls of museums and,
to a certain extent, in reproduction. Ballet enjoys no such advantages. The tradition is handed down from master to
master. Cease dancing for twenty years and the damage might
well be beyond repair. When the great dancer dies, nothing
but a name and sometimes a legend would seem to remain.
That is the superficial view. Tradition has been enriched by
every great dancer, and something of her contribution to the
art survives, and is taught in the classrooms and on the stage.
Taglioni, Zucchi, Pavlova have left behind them a very positive contribution to the art they graced, though it might be
difficult to analyse it in words. For this reason I have started
the book with a brief historical sketch. The average theatre-
goer may have seen or read a Greek tragedy; he will almost
certainly have seen a play by Shakespeare. The theatrical producer, the young Academy student, and the dramatic critic
will all be familiar with the drama of the past. It is rightly
considered an indispensable part of theatrical education. But
no dancing school teaches the history of ballet, few dancing
teachers themselves know the origin of the steps they are

teaching or their aesthetic significance. Yet such knowledge is both practical and indispensable. Physically, the young dance pupil is better trained than her actress sister; she works harder, she has more technical virtuosity. But mentally there can be no comparison. The actress from a reputable school is taught to think, the dancer to perform steps that are meaningless in themselves. '*Dance with your head,*' said Pavlova; the thousands of young dancers who graduate annually can only dance with their feet. The trade of dancing flourishes, but the art suffers. And it is important to-day that the art of dancing should flourish in this country.

Dancing knows no language barriers, consequently ballet is the greatest shop-window for a nation's art. What we know of Russia artistically first came to us through the Russian Ballet. We saw and applauded Karsavina; she showed us the art of Alexandre Benois, Leon Bakst, Nathalie Gontcharova, and others; through her we first heard the music of Stravinsky. The realization that Russia was not at that time a far-removed and semi-barbarous country may have turned many to Russian literature and drama. England has never been regarded on the Continent as a particularly artistic country, but now the Sadler's Wells Ballet has conquered the world and has paved the way for other artistic manifestations. A British Council Exhibition of British Ballet décors drew a crowd of over forty thousand people at Athens in 1953. I do not pretend that this was the best that we had to show in art and, in any case, it was shown out of context, but it was an introduction. To-day also students of every nationality come to learn ballet in this country. Ballet has become a national asset. England inartistic? She may lose international athletic events, but she has a high reputation artistically. The ballet, better than a hundred concerts or exhibitions of painting opened by epigrammatic ambassadors, can convince people of it. They will be learning without conscious effort. I have purposely stressed this utilitarian angle of ballet, since art for art's sake is not at this time such a popular slogan as art for propaganda's sake, and ballet is legitimate propaganda and not *bourrage de crâne* or a cominform device. To-day, in order to survive without subsidies, ballet must be popular. Its appeal is no longer restricted to the courtier, the specialist, or the snob.

After sketching the history of ballet from a practical rather than an academic angle, I will deal with the aesthetics of ballet, again from the practical angle of the dancer and her public. In a further section I will amplify that study by analysing certain 'key' ballets that are constantly in the repertoire, attempting nothing so rash as a guide to beauty, but filling in a background that may make the beauty more significant.

The story of modern ballet can best be developed by a study of various outstanding personalities, since an art of tradition depends essentially upon personalities and the impression that they make upon their followers, whose task it will be to preserve and extend the legacy. I will touch only lightly upon certain aspects of the contemporary scene.

The future of ballet will be decided during the next few years. All the trends and tendencies are there that will advance it as a creative art, and make interest in it a permanency or that will lead to a crash after the present boom. For this is a moment of boom, and my small knowledge of economics tells me that the word is an unhealthy one.

The teaching of ballet has become an industry, and even the dancing of that moon-magic ballet *Les Sylphides* is now almost mechanized. Day by day the subtle touches that made Diaghileff say that it had no *corps de ballet* but only principal dancers are disappearing, and with their disappearance prettiness takes the place of true romanticism, the prettiness of music-hall and pantomime ballet — A Glimpse of Fairyland, The Flower Garden Ballet, and such-like sickening spectacles. The ballet industry killed *ballet russe* from the moment that its talented but immature stars began to be quoted as stocks and shares. For the first time in history a very delicate art is in the hands of a vast public. Even the popular press has on occasions suggested how ballets should be cast, 'the management is unfair to the talented Mlle X and the lovely Mlle Y.' The ballerina, God help her, is news.

CHAPTER TWO

The Historical Background

The place and nature of ballet – The first important ballet – The birth of professional ballet – Technique and artistry, a permanent struggle – Noverre – The influence of Milan – The Romantic Ballet – The decline of ballet – The origins of Russian Ballet

I

THERE are various ways of treating the history of ballet: technically, socially, or aesthetically. The technical, while it is of the greatest interest when demonstrated, is dull and almost meaningless in description. I shall therefore refer to technical development but indirectly, and concentrate on the social and aesthetic aspects of ballet history. This chapter is merely a sketch with many omissions. Its purpose here is to serve as a background for what follows, and as a hint of the fascination and importance of the subject.

There is one initial conception without which it is impossible to understand ballet: it is the vital conception that nearly all young ballet dancers ignore. *Ballet is a modern art, dancing is prehistoric. The history of ballet is but a fragment of the history of dancing.* It may interest us the most, but it is far from being the most important. Dancing belongs to the village, the temple, the church, and, most recently, the stage. Dancing may be indulged in for the sheer pleasure of the performer, because the performer is frightened and wishes to placate an angry god, because it has become a ceremonial and the performer no longer knows its exact significance, because the performer wishes to entertain a public. Dancing may be entirely spontaneous – David dancing before the Ark; guided by a simple

17

pattern – the Morris dance; or highly complex and only possible to the specialist – ballet.

We are interested in dancing that belongs to the stage, that
has its being because the performer wishes to entertain a public, and that is highly complex in form and only possible to the
specialist. Such dancing existed in the hey-day of Greek culture, was known to the Roman Emperors and practised by
them, journeyed from Italy to France, and was, so to speak,
codified by the logical French mind to become the art we
know to-day.

Ballet, in the form that we recognize, had its being with
the founding of L'Académie Nationale de la Danse by Louis
XIV, in 1661. *We are able to trace its development in an unbroken
line of dancers and teachers from then until the present day.*[1]

The germ that was to develop into ballet was brought into
France from Italy by Catharine de Medici, who was eager to
divert her sons while she busied herself in ruling. The spectacle
was a combination of dancing, singing, and recitation. Its aim
was social. It constituted an elegant pastime for the monarch
and his court, an opportunity for bawdy humour, for lavish
expenditure, and for the fulsome flattery of court to King.
The subjects chosen were largely mythological; the King
played at godship, the court worshipped. Astute minds, bent
on politics rather than pleasure, used the fashionable craze for
purposes of national propaganda, among other things, to
point out to foreign ambassadors the might of France; much
as Hitler once performed his goose-step, but more elegant and
subtle, as becomes the French. The finest artistic minds of the
day contributed to the music, the decoration, and the poetry
of the spectacle. The people paid. The first dramatic ballet of
importance from which the history of the art may be said to
begin was *Le Ballet Comique de la Reyne* in 1581.

It was mounted by Catharine's first valet, Baldassarino

1. For the story of that pedigree, see the author's *Ballet Panorama*.

Belgiojoso, an Italian who took the French name of Baltasar de Beaujoyeux. He was considered the best violinist of his day, and for a long time afterwards the first violin continued the functions of dancing master. The teacher of dancing with his little kit is familiar in the work of Hogarth; Dickens mentions it at the class of Mr Turveydrop in *Bleak House*; Prince Turveydrop fiddled while his father revealed deportment. It was only later that there was a sharp division between the musician and the dancer, a fact that it will be well to remember.

This first notable ballet was to celebrate the wedding of Mademoiselle de Vaudemont, the Queen's sister, to one of the King's *mignons*, le Duc de Joyeuse. It told the story of a hero who escaped from the wiles of Circe through the intervention of the gods: a thinly veiled allegory. The ladies of the court, unaccustomed to dancing, which was almost exclusively a male pursuit, took part in what was the first *corps de ballet*. The steps of the dance being severely limited, de Beaujoyeux showed extraordinary invention in his pattern and production. 'Archimedes himself,' said Beaujoyeux, 'could not have understood geometrical proportions better than the princesses and ladies practised them in this ballet.' In planning a sumptuous spectacle to celebrate one happy occasion, he had laid the foundations of a new art form.

Under Louis XIV the dance developed still further. The King himself was an expert dancer who created an extraordinary number and variety of roles between 1651 and 1669, sometimes appearing in the same ballet under a number of different guises, from low comedy to an impersonation of the gods and heroes of antiquity. He enjoyed the collaboration of the greatest men of his day: the field-marshal de Bassompierre, a *premier danseur* between campaigns, so enthusiastic a dancer that he even worded a battle dispatch in terms of ballet, dignified parliamentary councillors and indolent courtiers who, devoting their whole time to the dance, became semi-professionals. Molière conceived subjects for ballets and advised in their production. Each one of his comedies contained dancing scenes, and many ballets introduced comedies. The two were not yet distinct. Lully and Beauchamps were the dancing-master musicians of the court. Already the art was becoming firmly planted in French soil.

There were professional dancers at this time: gipsies, tumblers and acrobats, rogues and vagabonds, wandering from fair to fair amusing the crowds with their capers, far removed from the elegants who danced to amuse themselves and their friends. To this day ballet dancers and circus folk alone in the theatre maintain a tradition of aloofness, living in a world of their own, true to their standards and beliefs. *Ballet as we know it was born when the acrobatics of the professional and the aristocratic grace of the courtier were united*. It was under the aegis of Lully and Beauchamps that the ballet became professional, and the change was marked by the foundation by Louis XIV of L'Académie Nationale de Musique et de la Danse in 1661, still flourishing to-day at the Opéra, Paris. The King himself, becoming corpulent, abandoned the dance eight years later and the court followed suit.

The dance made rapid progress, which students can follow in close detail, thanks to the notation of Feuillet, Thoinot Arbeau, and Rameau.

Now, the history of dance technique is closely bound up with the history of costume. The women's costumes at the court of Louis XIV were long and heavy, concealing both legs and feet. There was no chance for virtuosity. There could be a geometrical pattern, but no vertical movement, no escape from the eternal pavane and minuet. The whole history of early dance development lies in the search for elevation. When a ballet of this period required the illusion of flight it was necessary to have recourse to levers and pulleys; machinery took the place of physical effort.

The first ballerina to move upwards and so enrich the dance was La Camargo *c.* 1726, and she caused a scandal at the beginning by shortening her skirt just a few inches. The actual costume can be seen in Lancret's famous painting. She brought in the early form of the *entrechat.* Her great contemporary, Sallé, tried to free the dance still further by wearing Greek draperies in a ballet, *Pygmalion,* performed at Covent Garden, but the innovation did not catch on for two hundred years, until the time of Isadora Duncan. Only fourteen years later a pupil of Sallé was dancing in *Pygmalion* in Paris in a hooped skirt. The struggle between heavy skirts and muscular freedom continued until after the French Revolution, when Maillot, the costumier of the French opera, invented tights, and this hypocrisy meant the effective triumph of muscular freedom. Even the Pope sanctioned the usage of tights in the theatres under his jurisdiction, though they had to be blue so as not to suggest the too dangerous colour of flesh!

At the beginning of the eighteenth century, the five positions, basis of the technique of ballet,[1] known to-day to every week-old dancer, were used in a modified form, and Italian masters recommended a slightly turned-out position of the feet. For a long time French dancing retained the graceful, flowing, non-virtuoso inspiration of the minuet, while the Italians, given to the more violent tarantella, developed the athletic aspect. Although the two became rapidly blended, to this day the French style accentuates grace, the Italian technique. This history is not merely an isolated account of old happenings, but something that serves to explain the current scene. It is impossible to isolate the historical background from the aesthetic.

There is in every art a struggle between technique and artistry, the means and the end, the story to be told and the grammar and words used in its telling. Camargo had found

1. See Glossary.

PRE-CAMARGO

CAMARGO

ROMANTIC COSTUME

THE CLASSIC 'TUTU'

a new liberty, and for some time this new liberty proved so intoxicating that dancing became more or less confined to the marvels that could be accomplished by the legs and feet, hidden for so many years. Far-seeing critics of the period wrote that dancing had become so little expressive of anything dramatic that puppets and machines might easily replace dancers. The ballets of the time consisted of a series of danced entrances, scarcely connected by any idea; what we to-day term a *divertissement*[1] to distinguish it from a ballet. The means was so novel and entertaining that the end was totally forgotten, a state of things that will recur constantly in this history. *The history of ballet consists of periods of intense technical discovery and development, and then a pause during which some master-mind codifies these discoveries and shows their true use as an art form.*

II

The first of these master-minds, a major influence up to the present moment, was J. G. Noverre.

Born in 1727, Noverre is said to have been the son of an aide-de-camp of Charles XII, and destined for a military career. There is much doubt about the exact biographical details. He early became a pupil of Louis Dupré, and made his début at the age of sixteen. His first great success as a choreographer was *Fêtes Chinoises*, with décors by François Boucher. He was summoned to Drury Lane by David Garrick, and the great actor, who flatteringly called him 'the Shakespeare of the dance', undoubtedly had a strong influence on his work and outlook. Owing to the outbreak of hostilities between France and England on the first night of his London season, he was forced to beat a hasty retreat. This misfortune was typical of his whole life. As a man of choleric disposition he found it difficult to settle down, in spite of a success that won him the esteem of Voltaire and others, and for fifty years he wan-

1. See Glossary.

dered all over Europe, spreading his ideas through his example and more especially through his famous *Lettres sur la Danse*, published in 1760, a manifesto on the art of ballet valued for all time.

We can trace the influence not only of his letters, but of his ballets and of his teaching.

The theme of his letters may be summarized very roughly as follows: dancing, like painting, must be inspired by Nature. The choreographer is like a painter, and must follow similar laws of composition. If ballet is degenerate, it is because, like fireworks, it has been content to remain a pleasure for the eyes alone. Steps have become a meaningless formula. This is not the fault of the art itself. *The well-composed ballet should be a living painting of the drama, character, and customs of mankind; it must be acted, as moving in its effect as a declamation, so that it can speak through the eyes to the soul.* The laws of drama apply to ballet, which must have an introduction, a development, and a climax. If one had to summarize the teaching of Noverre in one sentence – I strongly advise all dancers to turn to his letters – that sentence would be: *Ballet is not an excuse for dancing; dancing in ballet is the means of expressing a dramatic idea.*

I will analyse and comment on this teaching at some greater length in the section on the aesthetic of ballet. From the point of view of history it is sufficient to say that ballet as an art flourished when Noverre's precepts were remembered and acted upon, and declined when they were forgotten.

Another great *maître de ballet* and theorist, Angiolini, had an acrimonious pamphlet debate with Noverre on the subject of dramatic ballet, and it is worth mentioning one of his points, which is of great practical value. He attacks the long written programme explanations of Noverre's ballets, which are indeed heavy and uninspired, maintaining that a ballet is a self-confessed failure if it requires a programme explanation to make it clear, a point that Fokine reiterated throughout his career.

As an active worker Noverre's influence was the greatest at Stuttgart, where he remained for eight years in charge of a company of a hundred *corps de ballet* and twenty principals, placed at his disposal by the art-loving Duke of Württemberg, Charles Eugene. 'You are a Prometheus,' Voltaire told him; 'you must form men and breathe life into them.' Stuttgart became a centre of ballet activity, and the greatest dancers of the day flocked there to appear in Noverre's productions, among them the great Vestris, Heinel, Dauberval, and Gardel.

Each one of these dancers has played an important role in the development of ballet which it is not necessary to trace here. Mademoiselle Heinel invented and launched the *pirouette*,[1] which Gardel and Vestris perfected, and they in their turn developed the *rond de jambes*.[1] To-day, ballet would be inconceivable without these movements in its repertoire. One of Noverre's most slashing attacks, implicit in his wish to develop pantomime, was made on the mask, which it was customary for dancers to wear. This was abolished almost accidentally by Gardel who, substituting at the last moment for Vestris, made it a condition that he should appear without a mask, and did so with striking success.

III

The most notable ballerina of this period, famous right up to the French Revolution and after, was Madeleine Guimard, 'La Guimard', who fulfilled all that Noverre expected of a dancer, subordinating technique to dramatic expression. The French Revolution brought a temporary halt to the development of ballet in France, though under the Terror the social dance flourished. The centre of interest became focused in

1. See Glossary.

Italy once again, where two brilliant men turned thoughts towards ballet and away from opera.

The first, Salvatore Vigano, 1769–1821, a nephew of the composer Boccherini and, through his master, Dauberval, in contact with Noverre's ideals, was a man of wide knowledge, who composed the music for his own ballets, which have been highly praised by Stendhal; too highly – he ranked them higher than Shakespeare. He greatly developed the use of the *corps de ballet* in the modern sense of the word, as an *ensemble* of individuals and not merely as a symmetrical background. Noverre had constantly railed against the deadly symmetry of the *corps de ballet*. Vigano's works and the trouble in France brought the leading French dancers to Milan, preparing the way for the second great *maître de ballet*. Carlo Blasis, 1803, a pupil of Gardel and Dauberval, is, with Noverre, the biggest figure in the development of ballet. In his *Treatise on the Art of Dancing*, he summed up and codified what was known, and his system is, in its broad principles, the one in use to-day. He is the father of classical ballet technique. He paid tribute to Noverre's aesthetic, remarking that only the technical portions were out of date. He was a keen student of sculpture and anatomy, and so lucid a writer that he was able to make clear for all time the mechanical basis of ballet technique. His best-known 'invention' is the *attitude*,[1] derived from Gian Bologna's Mercury. Both Noverre and Blasis stress the importance of a knowledge of painting and sculpture for the dancer. Their modern counterparts to-day, Fokine and Massine, are essentially museum men, as their compositions reveal, but museum men with an understanding, as Noverre insists, of the life that goes on around them. Blasis was a universal genius, a writer, and student of every type of art as well as of politics. His influence on the ballet is a powerful proof that it is not sufficient for the dancer just to dance.

1. See Glossary.

As valuable as his writings was the foundation of the great Academy of Dancing at Milan in 1837, a hundred and seventy-six years after the foundation of the French Academy. His rules have become a model that every institution has tried to follow. Pupils were not admitted before the age of eight or after the age of twelve; fourteen in the case of boys. They had to be medically sound and of good stock. Their training was fully mapped out; three hours' practice a day and one hour of mime. They were attached to the school for eight years, and after that their future was assured by an ascending scale of salaries.

This should do away with the superstition that it is necessary to start ballet training at the age of five, six, or even earlier – a super-stition that must have caused, and is still causing, untold damage. A parent who takes her baby to ballet class is an idiot; the teacher who receives her something very much worse. The baby can learn dancing, but only eurhythmics, or something of a pre-ballet type that is both healthy and of musical value. Apart from the physical damage, the mental effect of rigid ballet discipline at an early age is deplorable, killing origin-ality, spontaneity, and the essential joy of dancing. The great Russian ballerinas, who have set the standards for future generations, started without exception at the age of ten. This is but one of the practical lessons of ballet history.

Every boy and girl to-day who performs the arduous exer-cises at the *barre*[1] and in the centre is paying an unconscious tribute to the science of the great master, Carlo Blasis. Many of the teachers to-day, both Russian and English, are closely descended from him, since his pupil Giovanni Lepri taught Enrico Cecchetti, master of the Russian Ballet, and of so many English dancers. The thought is an inspiring one. The smallest pupil should have some conception of the dignity and history of her art.

1. See Glossary.

IV

The period that is best known to the layman through the many beautiful coloured lithographs that survive is that of the romantic ballet. These delicately tinted, highly idealized pictures of the great ballerinas Taglioni, Cerrito, Elssler, Grisi, Grahn, that decorate the rooms of so many of the dancers of to-day, have a great deal to tell us if we study them with care. No photographs could be so revealing. Cerrito floats over a waterfall, Taglioni walks among the tree-tops to gather a nest, moves across a meadow without disturbing a blade of grass. There are wings to suggest movement, never muscles. These charming drawings tell of an age of extreme artificiality, where the dance was used to exploit a new aesthetic, a period of great dancers idolized by their public, who forgot the art of ballet in their enthusiasm for the individual. The romantic ballet began in a blaze of glory, and in a comparatively short time burnt itself out, until only in Russia a serious public for ballet remained.

Noverre had postulated a close contact with Nature; romanticism denied it. The main influence of the romantic period was not a dancer at all but a poet, Théophile Gautier, a fact that has a very important bearing on the development of the ballet.

The romantic ballet was one aspect of a whole movement that swept over France and the rest of Europe, beginning in 1830. Its idols were Heine and Walter Scott, its greatest products the drama of Victor Hugo, the painting of Delacroix, and the music of Berlioz. 'Banish reality,' said the romantics; 'art must be an escape into an enchanted realm.' Revolution was conceived romantically, as in Delacroix' great painting, 'Sur les Barricades'; only later was it to be viewed solely as a problem in economics, persecution, pro-

tective custody, and mass murder. The ballet, ever a sensi.
instrument in the hands of artists, the ballet that created a
world of illusion, however realistically it was handled, was
ideal for the spread of romantic conceptions. The fairy, the
wili, the witch, and the vampire swept away the heroes of
antiquity, the pale German moonlight of Goethe replaced
Olympus. Man was no longer the hero, gone the days of a
Vestris; woman was idealized, and man must be content to
remain in the background and lift her when necessary – a
conception that upset the whole orchestration of dancing.

In the early eighteenth century ballet was exclusively a
male art, in the early nineteenth century man was on suffer-
ance. The romantics could not interfere too strenuously in the
technique of dancing, but since the dancer was almost an immortal, the technique did not greatly interest Gautier, and
at times he spoke slightingly of it, though as a critic he was
too great to admit indifferent work. The one great technical
development of the period was the use of the tips of the toes
– *les pointes* – the ideal taking-off position for flight. Ever
since the discovery of the points they have been abused, and,
more than anything, have brought the art of ballet into
disrepute with thinking people. I shall have a great deal to
say about this when I come to analyse technique.

The central figure of the period is a non-dancer, Théophile
Gautier, but the *maître de ballet* who translated its ideals was
Philippe Taglioni, important both as choreographer and
father and teacher of the great Marie Taglioni. None of his
ballets has survived. From all accounts his early ones were of
considerable interest, while his later work degenerated into a
formula that finally killed romanticism.

Marie Taglioni was a great dancer, unusual in her extraordinary frailty, that gave her an ethereal appearance. She is
considered the leader of romanticism; her ballet *La Sylphide*
stood for a manifesto of the movement, yet from all accounts

she was more purely classical than romantic, which presupposes a certain flamboyance that her rival Elssler possessed. Taglioni has been called 'the first Christian dancer', so free from sex appeal was her art, and slightly hostile critics even reproached her with being a dancer for women.

The fierce rivalry between Taglioni and Elssler did much to popularize ballet by fanning the spirit of partisanship that is known in every gallery queue to-day – and in the stalls. Of all the great dancers of that period, the one closest to us is surely Carlotta Grisi, creator of the role of *Giselle*, a ballet that is in the permanent repertoire both of our own Sadler's Wells and the Opéra, Paris. It has survived close on a hundred years, the only romantic ballet to reach us intact. *La Sylphide*[1] belongs to legend – its name is very charmingly suggested in a new romantic ballet that has rid itself of the conventional trappings and retained the spirit – but *Giselle* is fact. It links Grisi, Pavlova, Karsavina, Spessivtseva,[2] and our own Margot Fonteyn; Paris, St Petersburg, and London. If from our experience we talk of romantic ballet, it is *Giselle* we mean. I will analyse it at some length as a type of ballet, but this is the context from which it comes.

With the decline of the great dancers of the period, the popularity of ballet rapidly waned, for without these great dancers, what remained? The principles of Noverre were utterly forgotten, ballet was no longer an art but a spectacle for the eye of the tired business man, and the Edwardian business man could be tired, although the phrase did not yet exist. The ballet no longer interested serious musicians. The turning out of ballet music had become an industry. In every branch of art, romanticism was being brushed aside by realism, in its turn to be ousted by impressionism. The ballet had been one of the means of expression of a movement no longer in

1. This was re-created by Les Ballets des Champs-Elysées in 1947.
2. In Western Europe abbreviated to Spessiva.

vogue. The male dancer scarcely existed; just row upon ro
of pretty, grinning, well-corseted girls, a *foyer de la danse*
where the elegants could meet and flirt with them in the intervals, and a number of 'rats' – as the members of the Paris
Opéra *corps de ballet* were called – whose greatest justification
was to serve as models for the master, Degas.

Two hundred years after the founding of the Academy,
ballet in the country of its birth was artistically bankrupt. The
art that had been raised by a powerful dynasty of kings,
nourished by the genius of a Boucher, Boquet, Lully, Molière,
dignified by the interest of a Voltaire, that had produced
men of the mental attainments of a Noverre, had become
merely a prelude to flirtation, the dancers *grisettes* and expert
gold-diggers. It is well for us to remember that this occurred
but a decade or two after one of the greatest booms in its
history, when the attitude of the audience was very close to
what it is to-day.

The same was the case in England. The popularity of the
romantic ballet had spread from Paris. London was noted for
the warmth of its audiences. Théophile Gautier viewed them
with a certain amount of suspicion. He was not willing to
accept a London reputation without a severe test. There were
English dancers, but these were minor figures, the most
famous being Adelina Plunkett and the ill-fated Clara Web-
ster, burned to death when her dress caught fire on the stage
at Drury Lane. In England, without a State institution to
maintain at any rate the technical tradition, the fate of ballet
was still worse. It became a popular feature of the music-hall
programme, packing the Empire and the Alhambra. Many of
the dancers were excellent, among them Adeline Genée,
Lydia Kyasht, and our own Phyllis Bedells; but the ballets
themselves would scarcely have won the approval of Noverre.
They were the exact type of thing from which Fokine was
revolting, but without the academic purity that was some

justification. The ballet was rescued from this lamentable fall by the Russians, who invaded Paris in 1909 and London two years later, to remain in occupation ever since.

v

There is a mention of Russian dancers at the court of Louis XIV, when some 'Muscovites' came to learn the art and gravely displeased their teachers by their lack of attention. Dancing, however, received its first great impetus at the time of Peter the Great, 1672–1725. It was a part of his general policy to Westernize Russia, bound up with his costume reforms and with his forcing of the boyars to shave their beards. We have already seen the intimate link between costume and dance. This is but one more vivid proof. Dancing is the most positive and striking expression of the national characteristics of a people. Change their dances and you may change their mentality. In Russia the women were kept apart from the men. Introduce social dances, routs, and assemblies, make them compulsory, and Eastern seclusion must give way to Westernization. Peter the Great realized this just as Kemal Atatürk did in this century. Shave the men's beards, remove their dignified and cumbersome robes, and they become eligible partners for the dance. It may be necessary to imprison a few, to antagonize the Church. No matter. Peter was a dictator, and one of his aims was to impose upon a backward people the social dance of the West. The theatrical art of ballet has grown out of the social dance; the steps, originally performed for pleasure, are the basis of the classical ballet. In Russia, ballet followed the same evolution, more rapidly because there were examples from abroad. Peter forced the art of his country into a new channel, just as he forced the armament by land and sea. Where the dictators in Italy and Germany thought nationally, Peter, in every way a more enlightened man, had vision enough to think internationally, and to borrow what was best from abroad until he had planted it firmly in his country; painting, architecture, fashions, the army and navy. By so doing, he permanently enriched his country instead of impoverishing it in the present-day fashion ... *Alas, poor Salzburg!*

In the succeeding reigns, under foreign guidance, the art of ballet began to be planted in a country now conscious of the meaning of dancing. The Empress Anne (1693–1740) founded the Academy, which survives to-day under a different régime, importing a Frenchman, Landé, to direct it, and thinking it of sufficient importance to include dancing in the curriculum of the cadets. The Empress Elizabeth, a great beauty, was herself fond of dancing, and brought over an Austrian *maître de ballet*, Hilferding, with many of the latest works.

It was with Catherine the Great (1762–96) that the most intense development took place. Le Picq, a Frenchman, and the great Italian Angiolini came to her court and spread both knowledge and enthusiasm.

Ballet might well have remained a popular and 'borrowed' art, as it had done in England, but for one factor that distinguishes the history of Russian Ballet.

England enjoyed the art. The greatest dancers from abroad visited London and filled their pockets. Yet there was never a trace of a native English ballet until the present day. England remained 'good audience' throughout. Russia began to dance. This may be partly due to historical reasons. During the reigns of Henry VIII and Elizabeth the court enjoyed elaborate masks, but the growth of Protestantism in its puritanical form meant the decay of Merrie England, and one of the most musical of nations became a consumer instead of a creator.

In Russia, the court set the example and the people followed. The geography of Russia is responsible. The nobles possessed vast estates and quantities of serfs at their command, slaves of the same creed and race, who were not given their freedom until 1861. So large and remote were these estates that it was necessary for the nobles to provide their own comforts and amusements. The Empress favoured ballet, her courtiers followed suit. They trained their serfs and formed ballet troupes of their own. The whole Russian theatre owes its origin to the serf actors. This meant that ballet became a part of the people, not merely an entertainment provided from without. In Russia, ballet had a greater contact with humanity than in any other country. It could not be destroyed, as it had been in France, by any wave of artificiality; it could not become the very passive instrument of a group of poets. The peasant is by nature a realist, and Russian Ballet, even in its most romantic phases, has always retained, comparatively speaking, a close touch with reality.

Bit by bit these private troupes became merged in the central organizations of St Petersburg and Moscow, the dancers so selected gaining their freedom before the general emancipation of the serfs. The ballet school started as a system of patronage, but ended with rules as strict as those laid down by Carlo Blasis for Milan. The ballet became the most cherished possession of the Emperor, who lavished immense sums upon its maintenance.

From the time of Catherine onwards, the history of Russian Ballet consists of the gradual absorption of foreign knowledge by the Russians themselves until the art is indigenous and Russian Ballet alone exists as an active creative artistic force, producing its own Noverre, its own Blasis, its own Lully, its own Boquet. The succession of foreign visitors – Didelot, who had the greatest scholastic influence; Dupré, and Taglioni, who had the most enthusiastic triumph of her career – left not merely pleasant memories but a tradition that was assimilated. Russian dancers began to make a reputation, among them Andreyanova, who danced *Giselle* very shortly after its creation, the tragic Danilova and Istomina, sung by Russian poets.

Soon the stage is dominated by Russian ballerinas, Sokolova and Vasem being outstanding, though the guidance is in the hands of three foreigners, two of whom became completely Russianized.

Ballet in Russia became Russian Ballet through Marius Petipa, a Frenchman, Gustave Johannsen, a Dane, and Enrico Cecchetti, an Italian. The account of their influence belongs rightly to the modern scene, but before developing the story of modern ballet and introducing the major figures in contemporary ballet, it will be necessary to analyse the art itself and to postulate certain standards. Only in this way can we appreciate what is happening at the present moment.

CHAPTER THREE

The Aesthetic Background

Criticism – A definition of ballet – The dancers; their attributes –
Technique – The border-line between acrobatics and dancing –
Types of dancer – The choreographer; definition of choreography;
his attributes; nature of his art – Music and its possible relations to
movement – The décor and its function – The literary element;
theme and narrative

THE criticism of the ballet was highly developed during the
formative period, both by dancers and encyclopaedists. Up
till the time of Théophile Gautier, it continued as a serious
subject for study. Gautier's impressions of dancers are so vivid
that we can discuss Taglioni, Elssler, Grisi, and Grahn almost
as if we had seen them. Ballet came to be considered as too
frivolous for serious attention only during the decay of romanticism, when it left the opera-house for the music-hall.
The naughty nineties and the traditional draught of champagne in the dancer's slipper are difficult memories to live
down, obliterating the memory of such balletomanes as Voltaire and Stendhal. In Russia, where ballet never sank so low,
there were many remarkable writers on the subject, starting
with Volinsky, who learnt to dance at the age of seventy,
Plestchaeff, Svetloff, and André Levinson. They not only interpreted the finer points of the art to the public, but acted as
mentors to the dancers themselves. Their criticism was both
respected and feared.

In Western Europe, since the advent of Diaghileff, ballet
almost took its place once again as a serious and respectable
subject; the champagne-filled slipper was given a rest. However, in England and France ballet criticism became the ex-

clusive property of the music critic, and music is but one part of ballet. The dramatic critic, the art critic, or a critic of dancing might consider that they had equal claims. Though of them all the music critic is probably the closest to ballet, as a specialist he may well be biased; and while he influences public opinion, his other important function of influencing the dancers themselves is gone.

This difficulty of finding the appropriate critic will show us as a start the complex nature of our study. The would-be critic is still further handicapped by the fact that he has no score or printed word to which he can refer. He must rely upon eyes and memory, pass a judgement on music, choreography, dancing, décors and costumes, drama, and the combined effect of all these things together, for ballet is a combination of these elements. When he has noticed all these things he has a good half-hour in which to condense his opinions into two hundred and fifty words.

To understand ballet we must analyse each separate element, and we meet with an initial difficulty: that of where to begin. They are by no means in watertight compartments. It will be necessary for the critic to affix little labels here and there purely for the sake of convenience. Ballet is a particularly difficult subject about which to write, since it is quite impossible to make quotations.

It seems safest to start with a definition. I suggest the following: *Ballet is a form of theatrical entertainment that tells a story, develops a theme, or suggests an atmosphere through the orchestration of a group of costumed dancers trained according to strict rules and guided in tempo and spirit by the music against a decorative background; music, movement, and decoration being parallel in thought.*

What a cumbersome formula for anything so simply and obviously beautiful as *Les Sylphides*, or for anything so deeply and obviously moving as *Petrouchka*! Yet an examination of

37

this kind can bring out fresh beauties in each work by insisting on a certain standard of performance.

Let us start with the dancers, those partners in the composite whole that is ballet who are nearest to the audience, who interpret the music, the idea, and the choreography, and who wear the costumes.

A. THE DANCERS

Dancers vary enormously in physique, type, and temperament, but there are certain attributes that all require.

The first essential is a suitable physique. I hesitate for the moment to use the word beauty, though it is an obvious advantage, because beauty is altogether too vague a word. The modern sex appeal, too, is not accurate. One cannot and should not rule out sex from ballet, but the difference between ballet and some other forms of dancing is that they deliberately exploit sex while ballet does not, unless the theme of the work calls for it. Some superficial, smart-aleck or disordered minds have seen in the present-day craze for ballet nothing but sex, an altogether too easy judgement. For some types of mind the sex appeal of the dancers may be an inducement to visit the ballet, but they will find it in a far more practical and concentrated form in cabaret and non-stop variety, and are scarcely likely to become balletomanes on that score. The dancer requires the type of charm that a fair number of her audience will call beauty, and for a very obvious reason. Her face and her body are the instrument upon which she plays. While a violinist may possess both genius and technique, no one will be aware of the fact if his fiddle is poor in quality. He will spend thousands upon a Stradivarius or an Amati; the dancer must be born with the perfect instrument and develop it by training.

We have seen from our historical background that it is wrong to consider dancing purely from the point of view of the movements of the legs. The dancer must be completely expressive from head to foot. *The face is as much a part of the dancer's instrument as the feet and arms.* Many a dexterous performer is of no artistic significance owing to an adenoidal expression and a hanging jaw. Oh, those sylphs with their permanent air of acute bellyache, mixture of boredom and stupidity! Many a technical shortcoming has been compensated for by an expressive face that holds the attention. There are many hundreds to-day in the dancing schools who are doomed to disappointment because they have not had the good fortune to be built as dancers.

Under the heading of physical aptitude, I would include natural grace. The highly developed technical ballet dancer is by no means necessarily graceful. The highly trained dancer's manner of walking is often flippantly known as 'the *ballerina waddle*', a penguin-like method of locomotion. Technique can always be acquired, grace and ease of movement but rarely. Faulty teaching may ruin natural grace. *One of the aims of teaching is not merely to add something to the pupil, but to take advantage of what is there already.* Had quantity and not quality been the aim, Pavlova might never have had the opportunity of enchanting us with her art. Hers was a particular case, and every worthwhile dancer is a particular case, with an individual physique that must be studied and especially fitted into the classical framework. There is no infallible system; there are fortunately a few inspired teachers.

The next point to be considered is the pupil's musicality. It is obvious that she must possess an ear for rhythm. That is, unfortunately, the exclusive sense in which the musicality of dancers is usually considered. It is the bare minimum requirement without which the dancer is not fitted to appear at all. Its higher sense, the one which distinguishes the *corps de ballet* dancer from the ballerina, lies in a far more subtle understanding and appreciation of musical content and atmosphere.

The music speaks to the dancer, the dancer interprets the music to the audience. This will become clearer if I lay down a parallel with the legitimate stage. There the actress interprets the plot and idea of an author with words chosen by that author. The dancer interprets a choreographer's idea with movements devised by the choreographer, but an idea that never comes to life unless she receives guidance from the music. Let us take the extreme case of a completely plotless ballet, *Les Sylphides*, which contains the essence of romanticism with none of its hobgoblin trappings. There is nothing to guide the dancer here save the music. She is performing certain rhythmic movements, but that is not enough. She must convey to her audience a particular atmosphere. For that reason, only the truly musical dancer can succeed in interpreting *Les Sylphides*, one of the most frequently performed yet most rarely interpreted of all ballets. It is when ballet is understood in the Noverre-Fokine sense of the word that the dancer needs true musicality. During the degeneracy of ballet, when music is merely an accompaniment, the dancer requires but a good ear and a dramatic sense that is something apart. In the musical ballet, as distinct from the ballet with music, the ability to act and the ability to understand music are very closely linked together. The next point to be considered, therefore, is the ability to mime.

We have seen the importance assigned to this in our historical survey and the early distinction between the merely technical performer and the truly interpretative artist. Miming in dancing sets a difficult problem. It is, as we have seen, often closely associated with a musical sense; it is also rigidly controlled by the movements assigned to the dancer. Mime in ballet varies from the purely conventional sign language of the romantic period ballet (hand on heart means love) to the skilled acting of the Fokine dance dramas. It must never be thought of as something superimposed on to the movements of the dance, but as a part of the dancing itself. Miming that forces itself on the attention is bad, usually showing that the face is making a violent effort to compensate for the shortcomings of the body. When I come to deal with type ballets I will consider the isolated and exceptionally important case of *Giselle*. While this calls for very definite interpretation, every role in ballet requires mime, even when the *ballerina* is most herself in some sparkling virtuoso variation.

The other attributes required by the dancer before we come to discuss the problem of technique are simpler to imagine, more difficult to describe on paper.

Personality is a common attribute required in every artistic pursuit. In dancing it means style, movement that is controlled by the mind, instead of being a physical reaction prompted by classroom habit. Once again we are led back to music. *Personality in dancing, among other things, implies an individual reaction to the meaning of the music as against the muscular reaction inspired by the rhythm of the music.* It is astonishing to what a degree the dancer can become a puppet devoid of all personality, and yet earn tremendous applause from a public that can count up to fifty.

I distrust profoundly all superficial use of that much-abused word 'temperament', usually employed by the English public in its sexual significance to point out the artistic shortcomings of an English girl. There is nothing more deceitful than an assumed temperament that consists in making oneself seen and heard at all costs by a number of deliberate and unworthy tricks. It has proved the undoing of more than one dancer, who deceives a certain number of people part of the time. The Spanish dance is the one usually martyred by dancers who think a great deal about temperament: usually the English girl with an inferiority complex. *Temperament* in dancing, if it implies anything that can be analysed, *means natural vivacity and self-confidence, something that is felt with such sincere conviction that it becomes a burning necessity to convey it across the footlights.* In that sense it is an indispensable attribute that cannot be learnt. Let us be original and omit its customary sexual implications. Girls of all nations have lovers.

Intelligence is another attribute that the dancer of to-day more than ever requires. In the past the dancer received a true education as distinct from physical training. Music, painting, and the meaning of her art were analysed for her by experienced teachers. She faced her audience with some knowledge of what she was doing, a positive consciousness of the structure of which she formed a part. The present-day dancer, for reasons chiefly economic, is trained purely acrobatically. If she is to survive as an artist, it becomes vital for her to form a background of her own. The Maryinsky ballerina can discuss ballet; the average young dancer of to-day, steps. (A love of gossip is common to both, and to critics as well.) Lack of intelligence plus a lack of education condemns the dancer, after a burst of precocity, to complete artistic sterility.

I have purposely left all consideration of technique to the end. It is a complex subject that will need a quantity of convenient labels. *Technique is a means and never an end.* Most ballet dancers, and through them all the opponents of ballet, never realize that fact. It is vital, and should be printed on a placard in every schoolroom in the kingdom and solemnly intoned before the class. The numerous exams that are the goal of most teachers and pupils in England completely obscure that fact, making technique the end. Perhaps the exams are not to blame; there is much to be said for them, but their application and the attitude of the teachers is usually indefensible. Technique is sufficient when it enables the dancer to express with fluency both herself and the role she is undertaking. If she or her public worry about the technique, it is clearly insufficient. *Technique does not mean the performance, however perfect, of isolated steps.* The artist-dancer does not think in terms of steps, but conceives the dance as a whole, melting one step into the next. The dancer who reveals the join between the steps, the staccato dancer – and ninety per cent are – is as bad as the actor who stammers. Unfortunately, the public usually mistakes the staccato dancer, who underlines her difficulties, for the brilliant dancer. Applause is only too often a sign of the consciousness that something difficult has just been attempted. The truly moving passage is received with the rare compliment of silence before the final burst of applause. Unrestrained and unreasoning applause have been extremely damaging, especially in the beginning at Sadler's Wells, where the dancers were making a strong effort to sort out their knowledge of the art. There, applause revealed a strong tendency to become merely partisan. Sporting, perhaps, but unsound. The audience is showing marked improvement of late.

It is necessary here to pause and consider the difference between virtuoso dancing and acrobatics. Opponents of ballet as a system, such as Isadora Duncan, can see no difference, and often in practice there is no difference. *The difference between dancing and acrobatics lies not so much in technique as in a state of mind.*

It is possible for the same movements to be performed to the same music by two individuals and in one case to be pure dancing, in the other case acrobatics.

The pure dancer performs his steps, however complex, with the conception of the dance as a whole, being guided by the music, concealing his difficulties, and making his climax an artistic one. He is depicting a definite idea.

The acrobat performs his steps in such a fashion as to underline the difficulty of the task. In his case the drama is implicit in the physical performance. He is putting a question to the audience: 'Will I get through without a tumble or not?' He is telling them: 'Look, I am creating a record number of turns. Will I reach fifty?' That is the only idea behind his performance. His climax consists of a dazzling finish to whip up applause. There is relief in this climax that he has succeeded in overcoming his difficulties. It is like the singer of patriotic or Mother ballads who at the conclusion lifts his hat and waits. In the first case the audience murmurs: 'How beautiful'; in the second case: 'How clever.'

We shall see that in certain cases, especially in bad periods, the choreographer places an enormous onus on the dancer to steer clear of acrobatics, using difficulties just because they are difficult.

This consideration of technique is important just because the average ballet dancer is incompetent to defend ballet, either through words or dancing, against ill-informed attacks. The playing of the piano is well enough understood as an art for no one to utter such an absurd statement as: 'These eternal finger exercises are unnatural and dangerous to all self-expression. Let us throw overboard this elaborate technique and find something natural and simple.' Obviously absurd, but then virtuoso pianists have never been considered as particularly frivolous (no one has ever drunk out of their slippers), and, in spite of the popularity of ballet, dancers are still very much misunderstood and not accorded the status they deserve. The system of classical ballet is merely a physical training. There is nothing particularly beautiful in standing on one toe or in turning on that toe a given number of times. There is nothing particularly beautiful about a five-finger exercise. Beauty only comes later in the use to which these things are put. Neither is unnatural in the sense that both can be acquired with ease by the average person; both are unnatural in the sense that all art is unnatural and must be acquired through practice. It is through a misconception of technique that natural movement is always invoked in opposition to ballet. There is only one reply to this: ballet training is comprehensive, other dance training limited. The ballet dancer can perform every type of work: Spanish in *The Three-cornered Hat*, Russian in *Prince Igor*, Oriental in *Schéhérazade*, Greek in *Daphnis and Chloë*. Note that in not one of these ballets is the tip of the toe used at all.

The reason why the independent dancer of the Wigman type can make such a good argument on paper is a superior and bolder intelligence and education. In her devotion to a system the average ballet dancer has ceased to think at all, possessing neither taste nor discrimination. The Duncan or the Wigman, in elaborating a personal system, is compelled to study music, costume, and the meaning of movement. I do not for a moment claim that the great dancer must come out of the classical system. But what I do say is that the great independent dancer would be greater still if she had absorbed the classical system. There has always been a singular monotony in the work that has grown out of so-called natural methods; also, in most cases, the results have been so very personal that there remained nothing to transmit to pupils. The Pavlova of the *Bacchanal* met Duncan on her own ground, but she was also the Pavlova of *La Péri*, the *Dying Swan*, and that delicious nothing, *Noël*. Had Duncan possessed the fortifying discipline of technique, she would never have presented the pathetic and terrifying picture of her last days. She would either have been in a fit state to continue, or, by measuring herself against a known quantity, she would have realized the ruin she had become.

Technique is a known quantity by which the dancer can measure herself. A personally evolved technique, however complex, cannot serve that all-important function.

Dancing that gets its inspiration from ancient Greece is also popular to-day, and doubtless it is of distinct benefit as physical education. So is hockey. (Both have a thickening effect on the ankles.) Its artistic pedigree will not bear close examination. The dance rests on music. There is no one to-day who can tell us much about Greek music. To perform movements lifted from a Greek vase to the music of Chopin or Brahms is clearly not performing a Greek dance. The ballet has used on occasions the inspiration of Greek movement, but there is insufficient there to establish a whole technique, and the ballet technique has served its purpose admirably. It is necessary to have a very profound knowledge both of dancing and of choreography to knit the static movements on pottery and bas-relief into a connected whole. It is not sufficient to be photographed in draperies, draped round the Parthenon. Ballet technique may have its faults, but it does provide a tested and extended knowledge of the possibilities of the human body. It is necessary to state once again that a knowledge of that technique in practice must not be the exclusive aim of teachers and their pupils. The dancing rebels do provide one fine ingredient – thought. There is a close parallel here with the unlicensed medical practitioner.

It is not generally realized by the layman that just as there are types of singer – soprano, mezzo-soprano, and contralto – there are types of dancer. The dancer belongs to one type or another by reason both of her physique and, to a lesser degree, of her personality. Physique and personality are closely connected. In our everyday life the beauty is usually sure of herself.

The much-abused term 'ballerina' has a very positive meaning. In State institutions it is a definite rank in the hierarchy of ballet, just as 'general' is a rank that cannot be assumed at will; artistically and in practice, it means the dancer who assumes the leading role in classical ballets. The classical ballet will need elaborating in its proper place. I mentioned the difficulty at the beginning of this section of knowing exactly where to begin.

I can best define the classical dancer by discussing interpretation. All ballet training is classical, depending on the system codified by Carlo Blasis. That system is used for a variety of different ends: to express a positive role; to indicate an atmosphere; to interpret the national dance of some particular country. In the classical ballet the role is subordinated to the technique. Therefore, *the classical dancer holds us by her line and fluency and not by her interpretation of anything positive.* As we have seen, classicism and acrobatics could be considered as very nearly related. I have defined the essential differences. In classical ballet an enormous responsibility rests upon the dancer. She cannot hide behind her role. The music indicates the tempo, the choreographer the movement, the dancer is free, within limits which must be carefully appreciated, to express herself. It is she who must give meaning to what she is doing, since the story is told only every now and then by conventional gesture. The pleasure in watching classical ballet lies in the beauty of line and in the revelation of personality. One dancer may make her *adagio* exciting, another dramatic, a third ethereal, a fourth more tender, and so on. It is only in a classical role that the dancer can be dissected both as a technician and as a personality. Even the costume of classical ballet, the rim of a hoop, the *tutu*,[1] as it is called, is mercilessly revealing, nearly always unbecoming, and wisely abolished by Fokine. No frills, no bluff, no hiding of physical, technical, or artistic imperfections. Classicism, because it is all-revealing, is the point of departure for dancers and audience. It is obvious that the requirements involved are so great that the true ballerina is a rarity. Just because her body is her instrument and it is impossible to acquire one save by birth, the ballerina is more rare than the concert pianist or the violinist. There are no more than a half-dozen of front rank in a generation.

1. See illustration, page 22.

The good classical ballerina, unless she is limited in her mind to the interpretation of purely classical roles, has the necessary equipment to dance nearly every type of role. She is all-inclusive.

The next division, by far the largest and most common, is that of a *demi-caractère*. Here, the technique required is identical, its use is different. The *demi-caractère* dancer interprets a more definite role. As a ballerina, her role invariably has a name; usually she is a Princess; but that role does not require much interpretation, the dancing alone is the focal point. In *demi-caractère* it is the role itself. The dancer is a Columbine (*Carnaval*), a soubrette (*The Good-Humoured Ladies*), and the interpretation of the role is essential to the story. The dancer can conceal herself behind a story and a costume. The choreographer assumes a greater responsibility, he is partly a dramatist. Since there is a variety of different roles and costumes, both mercifully concealing, the dancer does not require the perfect dignity and physique of the ballerina.

The third category is that of the character dancer who performs either the heavily mimed roles, the villains and comics of classical ballet, the grotesques (Baba Yaga in *Contes Russes*) or the national dances (*Prince Igor*, *The Three-Cornered Hat*) of a particular country. England, having no national dances, is sadly lacking in character-dancers of this type, though English dancers excel in the heavy mime of grotesque ballet (*The Rake's Progress*). The attributes I have outlined apply in a varying degree to each of these categories. Karsavina excelled in all three – The Swan Princess, the Columbine, and the Miller's Wife. The outstanding young ballerinas, Irina Baronova and Margot Fonteyn, are also catholic in their capabilities.

At the present day, the tendency is for all dancers to be *demi-caractère*. The classical ballet is a survival, unfamiliar to the average teacher, and the secret of forming the true ballerina belongs to but a few institutions and those teachers who have themselves been ballerinas.

B. THE CHOREOGRAPHER

The choreographer (clumsy word) *is the person who, guided by the music selected, arranges the movements of the dancers, creating that part of ballet which is danced.*

It is astonishing how mysterious this profession appears to the layman. Many who watch ballet for the first time imagine that the dances are improvisations; in other words, 'just skipping about to the music', a phrase I have often heard. Even a learned judge and counsel in a recent case seemed to find some considerable difficulty in understanding the nature of the choreographer's art, and from various remarks that they let fall it was obvious that they considered it easy and of not much account, though they did eventually agree that it was susceptible to copyright. Actually, choreography is an extremely complex art, calling for exceptional knowledge, and the last fifty years have produced but a handful of choreographers whose work counts. To-day, dancers and public in London, Paris, and New York rely on the work of Fokine, Massine, Nijinska, Balanchine, Lifar, de Valois, and Ashton. The first four in this list have been active a very long time; Fokine since the beginning of the century. The greatest problem in ballet is that of the lack of choreographers. The reason will be clear when I have analysed the art itself.

To start with, there is no school of choreography or recognized method of training. There could not be, apart from the higher education of dancers in general. The choreographer is a dancer with a strong urge to express himself, the good fortune and the ability to be able to do so. He is born and developed, but not made in cold blood. The present writer receives a score of letters every month asking how to become a choreographer. There is no reply, even when stamps are enclosed.

The first essential is to be an active member of a ballet company, so steeped in the classical tradition that the desire for self-expression arises almost as a reaction against routine. It is necessary to be musical and to have a practical knowledge of music. It is necessary to understand painting and sculpture, both historically and aesthetically. It is necessary to understand the mechanism of the theatre and the spirit of the theatre. It is necessary to have a knowledge of human nature, the ability to inspire confidence and loyalty. Your dancers are like the artist's tubes of paint, with the great difference that they must be both willing and receptive. Is it to be wondered at that the true choreographer is a rarity? I must make it clear that this rarity does not imply that choreography as an art is equal to musical composition or painting. The rarity lies in the fact that *the choreographer, by the nature of his work, is halfway between the creative and the interpretative artist.*

There are many who arrange dances. To do that requires a certain technical skill, but it is an entirely different matter. To arrange a dance merely means the fitting of the ready-made phrases (*enchaînements*) of dancing into a connected whole. That is within the province of the good teacher. Choreography itself implies originality of expression.

One of the difficulties of choreography is its impermanence. In the early days, when the main feature of ballet was its geometric pattern, it was comparatively simple to fix the movements in a system of script. Even when the technique of ballet became far more extended but ballet meant two or three persons actually performing with the *corps de ballet* as a decorative background, the problem was an easy one, especially as the music was simple in rhythm. The movements of classical ballet were restricted to a framework that it is possible to describe in words so that a dance could practically be transmitted by post. Although there are a variety of systems of script, not one of them is yet in general use. Imagine attempting to reduce to paper such a ballet as *Carmen*, where there is no *corps de ballet* but a large ensemble of individuals, where but a few of the movements of those individuals can be described in words at all. The very idea of such a combined score of motion and music makes the head reel. Nijinsky, in the first throes of his madness, grappled with such a problem. The film alone could come to the rescue, a film that could analyse in slow motion, and already the cost of ballet is prohibitive. *Giselle* and *The Swan Lake* survive on paper, but the modern ballets run the grave risk of complete annihilation. They exist only in the memory of their performers, and in this lies the strength and the weakness of the art. Some central bureau for the recording of ballet, subsidized by the various companies, seems an essential in the near future. Already the Laban system of notation is being used in the United States for keeping a record of certain Balanchine works, neo-classics whose recording is comparatively simple. I still remain sceptical, although professional opinion has now swung round in favour of such recording. Apart from practical difficulties, I feel that the art of ballet would be the loser through becoming less ephemeral. The classics survive, but reinterpreted and considerably modified to suit each generation. The original *Swan Lake* reproduced exactly to-day would make the audience roar with laughter, and there is more nonsense talked about authentic versions than on any other subject. The non-classics have the comparatively brief life they deserve. Both *La Chatte* and *Les Biches* were masterpieces when created some thirty-five years ago. They expressed an exciting age of transition. When revived, they had no real meaning.

It is comparatively easy, by adopting some set of standards of the type I have outlined, to judge the individual dancer; extremely complicated to judge a ballet. There are so many factors to be considered. We must know something of the ballets that have gone before, and it is not always convenient to study several repertoires. It is impossible to form a very definite opinion, save of an obviously wretched work, except after several viewings. The musician will hear rather than see, the artist will study the grouping, the dancer the steps and their execution. For the average person it requires many visits to bring all these together. We can talk here only of essentials and see later how they have been treated in a series of type ballets.

The first essential, that postulated by Noverre and reiterated by Fokine, is consistency of plausibility. Ballet is a convention, we have seen that from our definition. The word need not disturb us. All the art that surrounds us has its particular conventions, which for the most part, through extreme familiarity, we accept unquestioningly. Perspective in painting is a convention, the convention that the two-dimensional has three dimensions; the bronze bust is a convention, and we are not upset by the fact that the human head and shoulders are gold, chocolate, or green in colour. The theatre has its conventions. We accept a play as realistic in spite of the fact that there is no fourth wall and we have no right to be looking in on the drama. The cinema has still more conventions, accepted by the millions who are ignorant of the word and its meaning. It is possible to be moved by the plot of an opera or operette, if it is skilfully presented. When you go to the ballet you admit ballet's own particular conventions, but you demand from the producer that he himself respects them and is thoroughly consistent in his use of them. In *Le Spectre de la Rose* you are moved by the young girl returning from her first ball and beginning to day-dream and then to dream in her chair. The fact that no young girl just back from a dance actually settles down to dream to music does not for a moment disturb you. When her dream, the rose she has been given, comes to life and dances with her, you are moved by the poetry of the conception, and you believe in what you are seeing. It has a truth of its own. But if that selfsame rose, instead of dancing lightly through the room, were to perform a vigorous Russian dance, you would be horrified and immediately lose your interest. The producer would, in fact, be a liar. This is not an extreme case by any means. Ballets equally ridiculous have been produced, ballets in Oriental or Greek settings where dancers have twirled on their toes. You do not demand accurate Oriental or Greek dances; doubtless, if you saw them, you would not recognize them. But you do demand something that does not shock your common sense. You know that a houri or a Greek maiden did not wear ballet slippers. You would be prepared to accept such a thing only in a highly stylized work that made a virtue of extreme artificiality, imposing yet another convention. You would then be entertained rather than moved. The essential difference between ballet and opera, on paper so similar by analogy, is that opera continually offends through the figures of the singers: mountainous women dying of consumption, ugly women assuming the roles of *femmes fatales*, fat head-waiterish tenors aping ardent young lovers. A part of Chaliapin's greatness was the truth he brought to opera.

Another essential linked with this is theatrical quality. Ballet which tells a story is a play which, as Noverre has told us, must unfold itself logically. Ballet is extremely limited in its choice of subject. Once it has found a suitable subject, that subject is susceptible of a variety of interpretations, actual and symbolical. It is possible to convey the fact that X loves Y, X hates Y. Then X may be Mars and Y Venus, X Mammon and Y Money, Power, and so on. The language of ballet is both restricted and extended. It is quite impossible to convey that X is Y's sister-in-law, and if the plot hinges on that fact, then the ballet is a failure. 'There is a quantity of things', said Noverre, 'that cannot be rendered intelligible through gesture. Everything that one terms quiet dialogue is unsuited to Pantomime.'

The choreographer, therefore, must choose only a theme that is suitable for his medium, and he cannot rely on the programme synopsis to save him. The ballet must be complete in itself.

Another essential that is immediately obvious in every other art is that the choreography must be the expression of a definite personality. It is personality, as we have seen, that distinguishes choreography from the arrangement of dances, however skilful. To judge of the originality of a work it is necessary to have had considerable experience.

The choreographer must use movements that his company can perform to perfection. It is useless to compose a work that calls for a succession of steps that only one exceptional individual can perform, or that the dancers can succeed in but every few performances. A good ballet is susceptible to a variety of changes of cast. The disturbing idea that the dancers may not be able to fill the choreography is immediately destructive of all illusion.

Good choreography must not, however, be interesting only because it presents an interesting story, it must be interesting bit by bit, in itself, through the use of the technique itself. Classical ballet, as we have seen, stresses line and purity of execution rather than literary conception. All ballet must be interesting in line and pattern. The dramatic content is one thing, the composition another. The choreographer is a painter with a foreground, his principals, and a background, his *corps de ballet*. This is an exact parallel, but it cannot be carried any further. It is comparatively easy to arrange effective groups. The choreographer's task consists in carrying the dancers from group to group. He is, in fact, painting thousands of different pictures, as a rapid camera will reveal. Each one of those pictures must in itself be harmonious. That is the essence of choreography.

To sum up, as far as we have gone, we have the following essentials: plausibility and a respect for truth; a subject that can be conveyed in pantomime; something original to say; a practical knowledge of technique; interest through the use of technique; a knowledge of composition.

These requisites are hard enough, but I have yet to tackle the core of the problem: the music.

C. THE MUSIC

Music in ballet can fulfil a variety of different functions. It can be the servant of choreography by merely accompanying movement, its most primitive use. It can be the master of choreography by setting the choreographer a problem, how best to devise movement that will interpret or parallel its thought. It can be the equal partner of choreography in which composer and choreographer jointly deal with a problem. It has been all these things. In the earliest days of ballet it is the equal partner: the choreographer is usually himself a musician. Then it degenerates into a mere accompaniment, a conception akin to the jungle tom-tom, or, earlier still, the clapping of hands and the stamping of feet, the dancer providing his own accompaniment. The choreographer designates a tempo, the composer obliges. With the advent of Isadora Duncan, and in the early Diaghileff period, music is the master. The music is already written, the composer dead, and the choreographer must fit his movement to what exists without permitting himself any liberties.

Diaghileff's ideal was to restore the equal partnership of music and choreography, which he did in *The Firebird*, *Petrouchka*, and a whole succession of works.

At the present time music is alternately the partner and the master: since the success of the symphonic ballets, usually the master.

It is impossible to lay down any hard-and-fast rules. Successful ballets have been created under each one of these systems. It is certain, however, that music composed for a definite purpose should in theory give the best results. Ballet is a whole in which the ingredients must be carefully balanced. Whatever the system adopted, it is essential for the choreographer to have a subtle and highly trained musical sense.

The question is often asked whether all music is suitable for dancing. There is a wrong viewpoint, survival of the notion that ballet is frivolous: that certain music is too sacrosanct to be touched. It is not a question of sentiment, but of fact. Much music, by its structure, is quite unsuited for the dance. A dancer cannot perform a solo of more than a very limited duration; the music may call for mass action where the story calls for a solo, and so on. In using already composed music there is a double risk: fitting a theme to it, fitting movement to it. Only in the case of the simplest or most formal music is this possible, or in music that has what Lambert, in an interesting essay, calls the quality of present action. Certain evocative music narrates and is physical, another type imagines. These distinctions are as real as direct and indirect speech, if less easy to define. However, the musical purist is apt to forget that ballet is theatre and must be judged by theatrical standards, and often his censure is true on paper, untrue in fact. I will discuss the subject of the symphonic ballets later. There is an interesting question as to the legitimate use of music in the case of *Le Coq d'Or*.

Le Coq d'Or was put on by Diaghileff in 1914 as an opera-ballet. The singers were stationed in the wings, the dancers held the stage and acted the plot. In this particular case it would be difficult to imagine a more successful presentation. *Le Coq d'Or* was revived by de Basil in 1937. Fokine, who had arranged the choreography of the original production, took charge of this, with the difference that the score was especially arranged by N. Tcherepnin, a pupil of Rimsky-

Korsakov, the composer, as a ballet. The singing was entirely cut.

The work, with its magnificent costumes and scenery by Gontcharova, was unquestionably a theatrical success, but certain critics attacked it on musical grounds. They denied the right of anyone to modify a composer's music after his death. On moral grounds they were undoubtedly right, on practical grounds only partially so. They stated that music composed for the voice could not be adapted for the dance, that the adaptation injured the music itself and was in any case unsatisfactory.

Fokine's reply was interesting. While it did not directly answer the charges, since in a sense they are unanswerable, it posed fresh charges.

'The libretto of Rimsky-Korsakov's *Le Coq d'Or*,' said Fokine, 'is based on a wonderful play by our great poet Pushkin. In adapting it the composer took many liberties with the verse. We must not forget that *Le Coq d'Or* is Pushkin's as much as Rimsky-Korsakov's. In my dramatic form I am restoring much of the atmosphere and characterization of the play.' In other words, he is telling the musicians, *Tu quoque*.

There were other arguments advanced, clever debating points, but they do not affect the main issue.

Undoubtedly a counsel of perfection would have been to commission fresh music round the same theme, but in practice the difficulties would have been too great. *Le Coq d'Or*, 1937 version, did offend musically, certain passages lost a great deal in value, and on that account alone it cannot rank with the choreographer's greatest. But it was a highly effective theatrical spectacle, and it did less artistic violence than a performance of the same work exactly as it was composed, but sung by fat singers with no conception of acting. In this last case, however, no music critic would have objected, and in viewing ballet the music critic is not always consistent.

The choreographer must have a musical conscience, the musician must understand that ballet is theatre, and often, for purely practical reasons, a compromise is necessary. This is no defence of music vandalism, but a plea of mitigating circumstances.

D. DÉCOR

We can best realize the function of scenery and costume in the entity that is ballet if we imagine performances of any of the works with which we are familiar in practice clothes and in front of plain curtains or a cyclorama.

Let us take a number of examples, starting with the romantic *Les Sylphides*, the very title of which makes us think of a dress worn by Taglioni, the direct inspiration of the work. Something would certainly remain, since the movement is beautiful in itself, but that movement was conceived with a special dress in view. The whole atmosphere of the enchanted grove would be lost. The gliding of sylphs would become the daily classroom exercises of flesh-and-blood young girls.

We can see from this simple example that while something of ballet still exists without costume (nothing remains without music or dancing), costume is not merely a pleasing embellishment added to the structure, but is a part of the structure. History has shown us the intimate connexion between costume and dance. In this case it intensifies the atmosphere from a dramatic point of view. The same ballet danced in the revealing classical *tutu* would immediately distort the whole conception by drawing the spectator's attention to the physical side of the dance, muscle and virtuosity.

The fact that the same movement in different costumes can convey such opposite impressions is a very striking example of the role that costume plays, and will aid us later in refuting a current fallacy. Our next example, *Les Présages*, is equally striking, and it has on one occasion been performed in practice costume. Yet, in spite of the fact that the way in which it is dressed is banal in the extreme, on that occasion the work lost a great deal of its meaning. The young lovers still made their effect, but the more positive character roles degenerated into exercises; Fate was no longer menacing, Frivolity was agile but not truly gay, Action lost in strength. These costumes were not good, but they contributed something vital to the theatrical effect.

In neither of these examples have I mentioned the actual scenery. There is a difference of function between costume and scenery. Scenery is something physically apart from the dancers and is less indispensably connected with the whole. It can save a weak ballet, almost spoil a good one, and add the finishing touch to a great one. Its primary function is to form a background that will show up the line and the subtleties of the choreography. In the first scenic version of *La Symphonie Fantastique* the backcloth was dark and the dancers sombrely clad. A highly complex piece of choreography, worked out in its smallest details, was entirely lost. The second backcloth was light and revealed the richness of the detail. It failed, however, to help the atmosphere. Had it done so, it would have been a complete success.

Another example is that charming ballet, *Jeux d'Enfants*. Here the story is vague and has little significance on paper, but is strictly logical in action with a truth of its own. Its logic is irresistible because action, music, and scenery move in the same direction. The décor here shows the valuable contribution that surrealism can bring to the theatre. Remove the painter's contribution and the 'truth' of this ballet would vanish.

The drop-curtain so frequently used must be properly understood in its relation to the work. It must not be merely an enlarged picture. It is a part of the theatrical illusion. If it is too violent or restless, it destroys the mood. It must create a sympathetic atmosphere and also induce concentration. It is parallel to the musical overture.

We have deduced the following: costume is very closely linked with the actual choreography itself, since it is physically a part of the dancer. Costume intensifies the atmosphere dramatically and so assists the narration. Décor must show up the detail and pattern of the choreography. Décor must parallel the music and movement.

This is a refutation of the easy idea that costumes and décor are merely an embellishment. Yet to-day, since the death of Diaghileff, nearly all ballets are mounted on that principle. Music and choreography are settled first of all, then the painter comes in and dresses the result. The painter has the right to be a partner from the beginning. Not only must the choreographer know the shape of the costumes, but also their colour. If grouping means anything at all, it is obvious that colour plays as great a role as line. Painter and choreographer are as closely related as choreographer and composer, and painter and composer are also related through the choreography as well as through the subject-matter. Only through such a basic conception will really great ballets be created. It is impossible to-day to touch *Petrouchka*, *Carnaval*, or any of the major Diaghileff successes. To re-dress them would be to destroy them. But most of the recent successes would actually gain by a change of décor, a confession of weakness.

A partial definition of ballet from another angle might be helpful. *Ballet is the result of a collaboration in which musician, painter, and choreographer interpret a common subject, each one in his own medium; the closer the collaboration, the better the result.*

Historically, the evolution of décor has followed very similar lines to that of music. At the start it is so much a part of the dance that it practically dictates the movement. The early choreographer, if he did not devise his own costumes, was capable of exercising a very close control. Then it degenerated into a purely mechanical embellishment from which Diaghileff rescued it. To-day it is well-meaning, but usually misapplied through lack of time and thought.

The early choreographers, Beauchamps, Noverre, Vigano, Blasis, were the men of exceptional knowledge in every branch of art. When the *maître de ballet* began to specialize in movement to the neglect of the other arts, it became necessary to replace his function of selection. It is this role that Diaghileff fulfilled so outstandingly. If décor to-day can be called well-meaning in principle, it is because Diaghileff educated every choreographer with whom he came into contact. Ballet décor is still entrusted to the interested artist and not the professional theatre designer of pre-Diaghileff days. What is lacking is the authority to guide the right artist once he has been discovered. Once more we are up against the old problem, the education of the dancer, and with every fresh confrontation it strikes us as being more serious, until we are forced to the conclusion that when all dancers can only dance, ballet will be in immediate danger of extinction.

E. LITERATURE

According to our original definition, ballet expresses *an atmosphere, a theme, or a story*. It is clear, therefore, that literature must play an important role, and the more precisely the exact nature of that role is understood, the better the ballet will be. A false literary conception at the start must kill the best of work.

Before the music is composed or chosen, the ballet exists as an idea. That idea is the common meeting-ground of the musician, the choreographer, and the painter. It is easy to generalize and to draw up some elaborate theory that will look well on paper, but it is better to deduce our theory from the actual practice. Daily I receive intricate scenarios for ballet; a few of them might possibly be suitable as subjects, yet without fail they are entirely worthless. No ballet scenario submitted from the outside has ever received consideration, and for a very excellent reason.

The modern ballet according to the Diaghileff system is not based on a concrete scenario. It is based on a vague idea that grows, develops, and takes form through contact with the painters, musicians, and choreographers, who are familiar with the medium. Literature does not dictate the form of the ballet. The immediate pre-Diaghileff method was to devise a scenario, like the plot of a play, and fit it with action, music, and costume. In the end, all that remained of the scenario was the story in the programme and some mechanical mime inserted at intervals. Words have a definite meaning, music and movement have not. There must therefore be a compromise, the nature of which will be evident when we select a few examples. I have already touched on the subject in the section on acting.

Petrouchka, the most successful of all dance dramas, had its origin as follows. Before undertaking *Le Sacre du Printemps*, Stravinsky wished to compose a work for piano and orchestra. 'In composing the music', he says, 'I had in my mind a distinct picture of a puppet suddenly endowed with life, exasperating the patience of the orchestra with diabolical cascades of arpeggi. The orchestra in turn retaliates with menacing trumpet blasts. The outcome is a terrific noise which reaches its climax and ends in the sorrowful and querulous collapse of the poor puppet ... I struggled for hours to find a title which would express in a word the character of my music and consequently the personality of this creature ... One day I leapt for joy. I had indeed found my title – *Petrouchka*, the immortal and unhappy hero of every fair in all countries.'

This is still far from being a ballet. Then Stravinsky played it over to Diaghileff. 'I played him the piece which I had just composed and which later became the second scene of

Petrouchka. He was so much pleased with it that he would not leave it alone, and began persuading me to develop the theme of the puppet's sufferings and make it into a whole ballet.'

With Diaghileff he gradually elaborated a story. Then Diaghileff wrote to Benois: 'You must make the ballet which Igor Stravinsky and I have in mind. Yesterday I heard the music of the Russian Dance and Petrouchka's shrieks which he had just composed ...'

Benois had always been interested in fairs, and so gave the ballet its setting, inventing the figure of the old charlatan from the inspiration of his favourite Hoffmann.

Accounts vary as to how the final story was arrived at. Actually, it was a close collaboration between the composer and the painter, each one of whom understood the medium of ballet, and of the choreographer Fokine, who brought final reality to their dreams.

This is typical of ballet creation, the translation into something concrete of a visual impression and not of a written synopsis.

There is the case of *Le Sacre du Printemps*, also revealed to us by Stravinsky in his valuable memoirs. 'One day, when I was finishing the last pages of *L'Oiseau de Feu* in St Petersburg, I had a fleeting vision which came to me as a complete surprise, my mind at the moment being full of other things. *I saw in imagination* a solemn pagan rite: sage elders, seated in a circle, watched a young girl dance herself to death. They were sacrificing her to propitiate the god of Spring. ... I must confess that *this vision* made a deep impression on me, and I at once described it to my friend Nicholas Roerich, he being a painter who had specialized in pagan subjects. He welcomed my inspiration with enthusiasm and became my collaborator in this creation. I told Diaghileff about it, and he was at once carried away by the idea ...'

I have italicized certain words to stress the visual origin of the idea. Nijinsky was also groping for a theme that would free him from the eternal use of purely classical technique, and so *Le Sacre du Printemps* was created.

Still one further example, this time of a very definite narrative to music already composed and for another story.

The origin of *Schéhérazade* is still under dispute, and for the very reason that it was a perfect collaboration. Prince Lieven, relating Alexandre Benois' point of view, writes: 'Diaghileff hit upon the idea of producing a ballet to Rimsky-Korsakov's *Schéhérazade* ... As a youth Benois had heard and enjoyed this music, and for some reason he had associated it in his imagination with the prologue to the *Arabian Nights* ... Rimsky-Korsakov's music was written to quite a different programme ...

'The conferences of the friends about ballet generally followed these lines: the music was played until it had induced in the listeners some *plastic image*. ... He (Benois) would fall into a sort of trance, shout to the others to keep quiet, and begin abruptly, accompanied by the music, to relate the appropriate ballet.'

It would appear from these accounts that the original idea of a ballet that grows into a narrative is arrived at by accident. That is not altogether correct. The persons to whom the ideas arrive and by whom they are developed are practical men of the theatre, soaked in the atmosphere of ballet and thoroughly conscious of the medium.

When ballets have been conceived by men of letters, those men have been poets, and poets in the *entourage* of the ballet. Théophile Gautier visualized the story of *Giselle* after reading Heine; Jean Louis Vaudoyer visualized *Le Spectre de la Rose* after reading Gautier. Jean Cocteau, who devised many ballets, is a painter as well as a poet-dramatist; Boris Kochno, a poet and an expert theatre man. The majority of the recent English ballets were devised by the composer Constant

Lambert, for so long musical director of the Sadler's Wells Company. There is no exception to the rule that the scenario devised in a purely literary manner is worthless. The actual workers in ballet must be fired with enthusiasm by some plastic image that is discussed and rediscussed until it takes on a definite form. To start with a definite form is to court disaster. Sometimes the ballet remains vague: *Les Sylphides*, the atmosphere of a sylph-haunted wood; *Carnaval*, the coming to life of Schumann's musical images; *Cotillon*, a ball with certain vague and mysterious happenings; *Jeux d'Enfants*, the fantastic secret life of toys; *Rendezvous*, greetings, partings, and flirtations; *Les Forains*, the contrast between tinsel and reality. In such cases music has suggested the atmosphere. In others it has been colour. But always it is the artist who has created the literary element of ballet.

There are two recent examples of 'literary' ballets that failed because the role of literature in ballet was misunderstood. I quote them; they remain as solemn warnings of what to avoid even if they do not survive for long on the stage.

The first, *The Great Detective*, was based on the personality of Sherlock Holmes. It sounds a good idea until we examine the ingredients. What is the atmosphere? Fog or drizzle in London. The sound of wheels on the pavement and the trotting of a horse. A bell is pulled, and someone runs up the stairs and throws open the door, revealing Holme's untidy study. How is ballet to tackle that atmosphere? Action there is in plenty, but it is not balletic – it depends on words as the puzzle is gradually solved, and on the gorgeous catch phrases that are so familiar. Holmes is more visually alive in the black and white illustrations of the old *Strand Magazine* than portrayed by a ballet dancer. The man is, in fact, anti-balletic.

The second is *Alice in Wonderland*, and here it is quite impossible to do more than give a series of *tableaux vivants* of the well-known character. This is a purely verbal wonderland, a work of literary genius. The most that can be done is to colour Tenniel's illustrations. Carroll cannot be captured. Alice, too, is anti-balletic.

Helpmann's *Hamlet*, on the contrary, is admirably conceived since it presents a purely visual scene, the pictures coursing through Hamlet's fevered brain the moment before he dies. Even the many versions of *Romeo and Juliet* are not too far-fetched. If they bear little relation to Shakespeare, they do at least succeed in portraying a romantic and unhappy love affair.

CHAPTER FOUR

Ballet as a Career

I

I HAVE in the last chapter treated the dancer as a part of the recipe for ballet. In the present chapter I am going to write of the dancer from an entirely practical point of view, and since there are countless thousands who want to be dancers this is an important chapter.

First let me set down some alarming figures that will shock us into being realists. One examining body alone, the Royal Academy of Dancing, has some forty thousand annual entries for its children's examinations. Obviously not all of them intend to be professionals, but the number is a large one when added to those from all over the Empire who learn. There are perhaps from twelve to fifteen vacancies a year in the professional companies. *It is, in fact, more difficult to enter the 'corps de ballet' of a reputable company than to gain a major scholarship for Oxford or Cambridge!* This means that, apart from a very high standard of talent and physical perfection, the candidate requires a fair share of luck; that is, of being seen by the right person, in the right place, at the right time.

I receive hundreds of letters every year from anxious mothers – there are a few fathers, too – asking how their graceful and talented daughters are to become ballerinas. There is nothing very positive that I can reply without a knowledge of the prospective ballerina. In countries where the only way to get on to the stage is through a state organization, the problem is a simple one – the organization either says yes or no. Here the leading companies have their own schools and, as they know their own requirements, entry into these schools is a help, but no company would refuse an outsider of real talent. The fact remains that, in spite of the numbers, there is still not sufficient talent.

Here then is a summary of the advice that I would give:

1. Is your daughter really well built: not too tall (five feet six inches is the beginning of the danger-point)? Is she strong and healthy?

If she is not well built, by all means let her study dancing. Careful teaching will improve her physique; but let her take up dancing with no illusions of a career, though there have been cases where knock-knees or bow-legs have been remedied in an extraordinary manner by a teacher who understands anatomy.

If she is delicate, consult your doctor, but experience shows that dancing is healthy. A career in ballet under modern conditions requires exceptional health.

On no account let her go in for slimming. If the hard work does not reduce her, then the cause of the fatness is probably glandular. Hard muscular work needs plenty of sugar as fuel. It is the mother's task to adapt routine and diet to the conditions of work. In England, where a ballet career is comparatively new and is a private matter, scarcely anything is understood about a dancer's health, which ruins more careers than any other single factor.

2. Do not neglect the rest of her education, particularly music. Piano is a definite asset to a dancer, and should be a part of her education.

The artistic child needs a highly disciplined education, and a background that can provide some sense of security where all else is insecure. 'Stage children' are a pest. The intending dancer should be a normal school child until the last moment, and should not be allowed to dodge the General Certificate of Education.

3. Do not stress examinations or become a cup-hunter, for reasons obvious in the text of this chapter. Examinations are only of value when properly understood, and are better taken late than early.

4. Once you have found a teacher whose record, academic and theatrical – and I believe in a teacher with a practical experience of the stage – impresses you, trust her and do not interfere or move the child from school to school. There are mothers who send their unfortunate daughters to three or more schools: unfair to everyone concerned.

5. Do not expect rapid results or be disappointed if she does not dance from the very start. The important thing is the correct placing of the body, upon which everything depends. This takes time, and nearly all present-day dancers are made to dance too soon; either because it flatters their parents' vanity, or because it is a pressing financial necessity. It is nearly always impossible to eradicate the mistakes of a false start.

6. About ten is the correct age to start; before eight it is positively harmful. Over twelve the pupil is a little handicapped, unless she is naturally supple and athletic. Over sixteen it is too late to hope for a successful career.

7. Always bear in mind that dancing is not merely something physical and apart from the pupil's reactions to everyday life. Character is revealed in movement to an extraordinary degree, as any psychiatrist will reveal. Meanness, arrogance, untidiness, shyness, fear, self-indulgence, slyness, lack of discipline are all traits that are speedily revealed in the dance. Therefore the parent has as much control of the pupil as the teacher, and can touch certain springs hidden to the teacher. Often the parent undoes the excellent work of the dancing school, by imagining that the budding genius

requires very special treatment, instead of a thoroughly normal disciplined life on common-sense lines. I know of numberless examples, which every teacher can confirm, of good material ruined by misplaced affection.

The mother should not sit and watch every movement of the class, as so many do. It would be equally ridiculous to watch the son's Geography or Latin lessons. The same point of view applies to each case.

The ballet mother has been notorious for the past hundred years. Albert Smith, author of an amusing pamphlet published in 1857, *The Natural History of the Ballet Girl*, writes: 'The Ballet Girl has more frequently a mother than a father; a singular provision of Nature appears to have denied the latter parent to them ... But they have all got mothers ...'

8. The making of a dancer is an expensive business. In cases of exceptional talent, the really good teacher will make considerable reductions. A successful pupil is her finest advertisement. Also, there are various scholarships and local education authorities' grants available.

9. To join a company requires perseverance, patience, exceptional ability, and good fortune. If you aim at a career in ballet for your daughter, you must be an idealist, for a ballet career in the ordinary course of events is not a practical aim. The openings are too few and the rewards too small.

10. There are various by-products of ballet training that should be borne in mind. It is a good preliminary to all stage work, especially to-day when the dancer in musical comedy or in films must be ballet-trained. There are also many good openings in teaching, and the Royal Academy of Dancing has an excellent Teachers' Training course – which is not, however, for the failed dancer but for the girl with a real vocation.

11. Finally, the work is worth doing for its own sake.

II

To-day, the average girl works chiefly for exams – those of the Royal Academy of Dancing and other bodies. These exams are carefully arranged, but in practice they can be as harmful as they are beneficial. They must be put in their right perspective.

They bear no relationship whatsoever to the prospects of success in a ballet company – neither Markova nor Fonteyn hold any certificates – all that they can tell one is that the pupil has mastered a certain technique, which does not mean that she is a dancer. They are in a sense more a control of the teacher than of the pupil, and in that way they have done much good. The harm that they have done when misunderstood is immense. First of all they are usually taken far too young, and pupils and teachers are so buried in a syllabus that dancing does not enter into the matter at all. The exams should be taken in the pupil's stride with no need for cramming, and, most important of all, the pupil should be properly 'placed' – and that takes time – before studying a more advanced technique. There should, too, be a distinction between the future professional and the amateur or the would-be teacher.

There is a vast difference in the approach, and for the most part examining bodies are still working in the dark. This suits the unimaginative teacher, who earns a living by sticking slavishly to a syllabus, where successes bring her more and more pupils. What is needed is a simple, independent board of examiners, whose members have real artistic experience, are completely unhampered by schools of their own, and know exactly for what they are looking. Until that comes about, dancing examinations will not be taken very seriously either by education authorities, who are wonderfully sympathetic to ballet training and eager to assist in the discovery of talent, or by practical people of the theatre.

Dancing competitions are an unmitigated evil from every point of view. The winner imagines that she has great talent, while the loser thinks that she has been unfairly treated. If dancing is an art, it cannot become a matter of cup and medal hunting. These things involve much time off from school, considerable strain, and in my experience succeed in spoiling more dancers than anything else.

III

This book stresses ballet as an art for professionals, but it is important to mention its educational side as far as it concerns what one might call 'the once-a-week child'. To-day most children learn some form of dancing, and everyone realizes that gymnastics are not a substitute. A few are beginning to realize that the gymnastics teacher is not the best person to teach dancing, even if she has had a few months' training in one of the modern methods that are so rapidly out of date. Dancing is a wonderful activity, but to be of any value it must be based on a sound and proved technique. Children enjoy rules; their own games have more rules than any grown-up would dare to impose. For a time it was thought wonderful to let children express themselves freely to percussion or, more rarely, to music. It was supposed to act as a release, though I never found out what it released. I am old fashioned enough to believe that certain primitive emotions are best suppressed, and much of the modern dance seems to me psychologically morbid and unhealthy. The basic technique of ballet, together with simple dances, mime, and rhythmic movement, forms a wonderful education. It develops self-discipline, co-ordination, and quick thinking, a sense of music, grace, and health. The Royal Academy of Dancing's Ballet in Education has much that is really valuable when the syllabus is used as a very rough guide to the standard required, and then interpreted by a clever teacher to suit the needs of her pupils. Alas, too often it is made into a dreary and over-technical preliminary to senior examinations, and its whole value is lost. The dancing profession is still in the stage of looking upon examinations as a virtue in themselves, and of multiplying instead of curtailing them.

Also the conception of ballet in education is so new that there are not yet enough really qualified teachers. What is essential is for the teacher to realize that she is teaching children and not just steps, also that unlike the teacher of the professional child she must concentrate on the most unlikely material, and find it a triumph and a reward in itself when the shy child joins in the class, the naughty child obeys the word of command, and the uncoordinated child ceases to trip and stumble.

The Royal Academy of Dancing has an admirable three years' Teachers' Training Course, which seeks to form the teacher from that point of view. Girls from seventeen years of age who have passed their Elementary Royal Academy exam and their General Certificate of Education in five subjects are eligible. This whole thing is still in a pioneer stage, but much has been learnt in the past ten years, and the educational world has gone more than half-way to meet the dancers.

Finally, Dalcroze Eurhythmics is a wonderful system of musical education for all children, whether they intend to be professionals or merely to dance for pleasure. It is not a substitute for dancing, nor was it ever intended to be so. I would say that for the under nines it is the perfect beginning; it could be of even greater value if the Eurythmics people as a whole paid closer attention to posture.

CHAPTER FIVE

Founders of Twentieth-Century Ballet

I. SERGE DIAGHILEFF

The reign of an absolute monarch

I

THE history of ballet is continuous: it travels from country to country, Italy to France, France and Italy to Russia, Russia to England; but it remains in the hands of those who have inherited the tradition. There is evolution but never revolution; progress is gradual and not forced. It is difficult to judge where exactly the history of modern ballet begins. I left my historical survey with the advent of three foreigners – Petipa, Johannsen, and then Cecchetti – to Russia. The effect of that arrival truly starts the story of modern ballet as we know it in practice to-day.

Petipa, a Frenchman from Marseilles, had a unique opportunity in which to found a school, having charge of the same company for some fifty years, and mounting on them fifty-seven full-length ballets in all as well as supervising all the work that was done. Neither Noverre nor Blasis, superior in every way as thinkers, had such a chance to exercise and develop his craft.

As a teacher, Johannsen enjoyed similar opportunities, bringing with him the pure French school which the French themselves were beginning to forget. Soon there was a whole generation of Russian-born dancers, where formerly they had been exceptions.

Work under one *maître de ballet*, however gifted, over a long number of years becomes monotonous, and after a quarter of a century Petipa was beginning to work by formula. The dances themselves were also getting into a groove when the Italian Cecchetti appeared in a private theatre with an Italian company. Grace and elegance were characteristics of the French, strength and virtuosity of the Italians, and it was their virtuosity that appealed to the public. Greatly daring, the then director of the Imperial Theatres, A. Vsevolojsky, engaged Cecchetti as a *maître de ballet*. Cecchetti was a teacher of genius. The new Italian method plus the rivalry caused by the two schools brought something new and vital, giving birth to a Russian method, *three-quarters French school and a quarter Italian school seen through the Russian temperament and shown through the Russian physique*. That is the exact meaning of that much-abused term *Russian Ballet*. English Ballet, about to be born as a method, will consist of the Russian school seen through the English temperament and shown through the English physique. It is already beginning to take shape, too embryonic as yet to characterize and label in the inexactly exact manner so beloved of critics.

In addition to engaging Cecchetti, who supplied the ingredient missing in Russian Ballet, Vsevolojsky commissioned ballets from Tchaikovsky, interesting after a very long interval the original musician in the medium of ballet.

But in every art a period of great perfection gives way to a sterile academism. A Raphael and a Michelangelo arise, leaving behind both beauty and an impossible path to follow. Their genuine personal discoveries become laws, the form of their work is followed but not its spirit. And they must wait fresh discovery at a later period when criticism allows them to be valued afresh. The formula of their work is repeated when its meaning is no more. Sometimes a veteran seeks to repeat his own early successes with the same result. Petipa was a veteran. By 1900 he had served the theatre fifty years, accomplishing a gigantic task. His work, thanks to the wise guidance of Vsevolojsky, had undergone one renaissance, but he had reached the end. Though ballet had never reached the low ebb of France, had never degenerated to the music-hall, as in England, there was nothing in it of interest for the thinking man. The conservative balletomane sat in his front row, peered and applauded, criticized, compared, and applauded. He did not wish for a change; he, too, had become a somewhat quaint survival. Ballet and balletomanes were museum exhibits.

There were great dancers who often shone in works unworthy of them – Kchesinska, sparkling virtuoso outstanding in *Esmeralda*; the perfectly classical Trefilova; Preobrajenska, witty, and the idol of the gallery; Egorova and others. While Pavlova travelled, they earned the plaudits of the balletomanes at home.

The renaissance of dancing has been theirs. As *émigrées* forced to spend their retirement teaching in Paris, they have formed the whole present generation of Russian dancers.

Isadora Duncan came to Russia and caused a sensation. She wore the flowing draperies that Sallé had vainly attempted to introduce two centuries before. She discarded the ballet shoe, sacred symbol of the art of dancing. More daringly she danced to music that had been heard only in the concert-hall and that the majority of the balletomanes were quite incapable of understanding. She tried to interpret the meaning of that music in her dances. Technically she was a revolutionary, artistically, as we know, she was returning to the first principles of ballet.

She expressed herself as horrified by the artificialities of ballet, she praised and patronized individual dancers. Her advent would have made little permanent impression had others connected with the academic body itself not felt exactly the same.

Michel Fokine, a graduate of both the Imperial and dramatic schools, a musician and a painter, was undergoing a process similar to that of Duncan. He was not a revolutionary in her sense, for he valued the tradition and the training out of which he was born, and wished to preserve what was best. His aim was to resume where Noverre and Blasis had left off. Duncan was horrified by what she saw, and, illogically, blamed the whole art for the manner in which it was being used. Fokine approved of the basis of the art, but wished to find a different application in which nature could become once again the guiding inspiration. She objected to the use of the points in dancing, he to the abuse of the points. She and her followers exaggerated their importance just as the ballet was doing.

His first step was to abolish the enormously long entire evening ballet. To him, ballet must express itself with economy, not pretend to tell a story and then proceed to ignore it. Theme, atmosphere, correct style, were the things that truly mattered. His first ballets, *Nuits d'Egypte* and *Eunice*, while they earned the admiration of the wise old man, Petipa, caused such an uproar that they nearly drove him from the theatre. Here was the tradition that they had established with such care and expense being destroyed by a young upstart. But it was he who understood the true tradition, not they. The fellow was actually making ballerinas dance on their bare feet, and upsetting the sacred order of things so completely that one could no longer tell at what period in the ballet the 'high spot' of the evening occurred. These were indeed infamies, said the ballet Blimps.

Fokine might have abandoned the dance altogether if artists in other media had not been following a parallel path and did not see in ballet the perfect medium for the music and art in which they were interested.

II

The leader of this group of earnest young thinkers was Alexandre Benois, a man of encyclopaedic knowledge in every branch of art and literature, the descendant of a long line of artists, painters, and architects. His maternal grand-father was a composer, his uncle a distinguished theatrical architect.

As a student at school he had already gathered round him a group of friends, and later, at the university, they formed themselves in a club in which each one lectured on his own particular subject.

It is a characteristic of Russians to discuss endlessly until they have talked the original subject completely away, pre-ferring dreams to reality, and Benois' group might easily have done the same, though Benois himself was a creative artist, had it not been for the advent of Serge Diaghileff, a country cousin of one of them.

Serge Pavlovitch Diaghileff was born at Perm in 1872. He belonged to the country nobility, an important factor in discussing his character. His environment was one of ease and culture, in which music and theatricals played a large part. It was his ambition to become a composer, but he came to St Petersburg to study law at the university.

From the first he was different from the little group sur-rounding Benois. They considered him to be definitely pro-vincial, less cultured than they, and, in spite of that, a little too bumptious and aggressive. They were definitely smug. He did not at first belong to the inner circle; he was on the fringe of the group purely through the accident of cousinship.

His university career was a secondary consideration. He went to the theatre, the opera, and to concerts, and developed his music, though early on he met with a check when Rimsky-Korsakov told him that he did not have an original talent. He is said to have retorted with supreme self-confi-dence, 'I will be remembered when you are forgotten.' He did much to make Rimsky-Korsakov remembered. He travelled, visited studios and museums, and in conversation with friends sharpened his critical faculties. He was an enthusiast able to communicate his enthusiasm. Soon he became the leader of the group, the man who could put their theories into practical reality.

It was natural that, with so much to express, the friends should turn to journalism, and under the editorship of Diaghileff and Benois they started *The World of Art* (*Mir Isskoustva*). The difficulties of the undertaking were enormous. Russia was behindhand in artistic book production, and it was necessary to find the plant from abroad and to create the journal physically as well as artistically. This and the organization of a series of art exhibitions proved Diaghileff's abilities as an active organizer, and taught him the first essentials of an impresario, though the term describes only a small part of his true function.

The platform of *The World of Art* was individualism. 'One of the greatest merits of our times,' wrote Diaghileff, 'is to recognize individuality under every guise and at every epoch.' He defined art as a 'free and disinterested act taking place in the soul of the artist'. 'The sole function of art is pleasure, its only instrument beauty. ... It is blasphemous to force ideas.'

He maintained that art should exist for art's sake and not to teach a practical lesson. It could have no concern with earthly difficulties. He attacked both didactic art and sterile academism, making himself a host of enemies.

III

It is only natural that with such a reformer's platform, ballet should appear as an ideal medium and one in which the quickest results could be obtained. They had within their own group the necessary painters and musicians, and the young choreographer Fokine was burning for an opportunity to express himself.

During his first years in St Petersburg, Diaghileff was not interested in ballet, seeing only the ridiculous artificialities that had it in a stranglehold. Benois and his friend Nouvel, through seeing an exceptional dancer, Virginia Zucchi, were the only confirmed balletomanes, and it was they who turned Diaghileff's thoughts in that direction.

The friends seemed to have gained their opportunity almost without a struggle when Diaghileff was offered an administrative post in the Imperial Theatres by a director eager for reform, Prince Serge Wolkonsky. Both through the journal and his conduct of the theatre Diaghileff had made many enemies. He was completely uncompromising. The production of Delibes' *Sylvia* was to be entrusted to him when those enemies revolted and, addressing a deputation to Wolkonsky, refused to have anything to do with the production. Wolkonsky, faced with a strike, countermanded the production. Diaghileff insisted and was dismissed. A year later, Wolkonsky himself resigned after an administrative dispute, and the key post of director of the Imperial Theatres fell into the hands of a reactionary, Teliakovsky, an avowed enemy of Diaghileff and the group. All hopes of successful experiments in ballet in Russia were dead.

Diaghileff continued to organize exhibitions with great success, brought Russian painting, music, and opera to Paris, but never ceased to dream of ballet.

Finally, in 1909, after conquering innumerable difficulties, many of them provoked by his own uncompromising attitude, he brought a Russian company to Paris, where its success revolutionized the history of ballet in Western Europe and later in America, leaving only his own country out of it, until to-day in Russia, country of the successful revolution, the tradition of Petipa continues almost unchanged, though a commissar may sit in the box of an Emperor.

IV

To understand the character of the new Russian Ballet it is necessary to understand the character and artistic evolution of its founder, for the ballets he presented were the expression of his artistic tastes of the moment. Save with Gautier, and Gautier's influence was far less, there is no one who can be compared with Diaghileff, non-dancer, non-composer, non-artist, who influenced the ballet, the music, and the art of his whole period.

The first conception we must have is that of the nobleman. The Russian noblemen had their own troupes, who performed for their pleasure and for that of their friends. Diaghileff was the direct descendant of such serf-owning nobles, and it coloured his attitude. He was first of all a man who indulged his own personal tastes and graciously allowed his friends to share his pleasure, and only afterwards a business man interested in such prosaic affairs as the box-office. To-day the box-office must rule, and we can no longer look at the ballet in the same way. Diaghileff represents the bridge between monarch and business man. Only after him does ballet become truly democratic.

Though Diaghileff was an autocrat he never attempted to dispense with advisers, and he had the flair for discovering new collaborators throughout his career. We have examined the ingredients that compose ballet, and since nowhere does the role of a Diaghileff appear, one must ask oneself exactly in what it consisted.

He created the role, it was a part of his mental make-up. He was a Maecenas who did not spend his own money, an impresario who ignored the public taste, a business man who lost money: all these are negative things. As he never wrote or talked about himself we must deduce the positive ones. I have asked the majority of his collaborators to enlighten me, and their usual reply is a vague one that assigns to him some organizing role or other and leaves the creative side to them. This is not so much a question of jealousy as of ignorance. They were the medium in which Diaghileff worked. Someone in his *entourage* would suggest an idea at supper, the idea would appeal to him. He would think of a composer and painter and introduce the idea to them. They would discuss it, with Diaghileff there to prompt and encourage them, then in a few months' time, in some cases a few years, a ballet would be ready. By that time no one could say whose was the original idea, and there was no trace of Diaghileff's work; but it was he who prevented the idea from being swept away with the remains of the meal and who found the very people who could develop it.

Once it had become a production his function became that of censor. Before he had acted through flair, now it was through knowledge. He criticized music, both the composition and the execution, and musicians listened to him with respect and the minimum of anger. He modified a costume, suggested a change in the colour scheme, and so on. The dancing alone he did not touch, but he influenced the choreographer during the months in which the work was in question. Added to his flair was a passion for education. He discovered a 'genius', a word that he was fond of using, then took him to museums and concerts, brought him into contact with artists, moulding his opinions and trying to mould his character. So that, even though his name appears on no programme opposite a specified function, every production bore the imprint of his personality. The one role which he readily admitted was that of lighting expert. He had an extraordinary knowledge of theatre lighting and endless patience, spending as much as twelve hours on a set, until he had reached perfection. To-day, it is all done within an hour, and, unfortunately, all too often conveys that impression. The essence of a Diaghileff production was its unity and the close attention to minute detail, at times extravagant and unnecessary.

His taste varied as we shall see when we discuss his work and there seems a contradiction at times in the character of the cosmopolitan who was a patriot, the lover of Tchaikovsky, who belonged to the *avant-garde*, the romantic, who showed us *Le Pas d'Acier*: a contradiction that has raised doubts as to his sincerity. There is not the space here to trace bit by bit the happenings of his private life and their influence on his work; also it is not within the scope of this book. The one important thing to note is that it can be done and that it shows beyond doubt that the Diaghileff Ballet was Diaghileff.

Diaghileff was all his life terrified of death, admiring intensely everything that was young and vital. It is that quest for youth, growing feverish as he advanced in years, that accounts for the frantic modernism of the last phase, and all the time there was a deep natural love of the classicism and romanticism that reminded him of his own youth and the resultant conflict between the two. That is the only way in which we can truly understand Diaghileff.

Much has been written about his brutality and the manner in which he treated Nijinsky. This does not concern us here, though it must have altered the course of ballet history. An art such as ballet, where the tradition belongs to but a few people at one time and in one place – and during the twenty-five years the living art of ballet was travelling with Diaghileff, a part of his baggage – is constantly being influenced by private relationships. Diaghileff was domineering: no mild-mannered man could have kept the company alive throughout the 1914 War; but some of the portraits that had been painted of him as a scheming, medieval villain are ridiculous and not borne out by facts, which show that he was loyal to his collaborators, with certain exceptions, thoughout his long reign.

He was no Svengali, and those collaborators were neither mediums nor puppets, but thinking, intelligent beings, the finest artistic minds of the age, whom he stimulated and inspired: a different matter altogether. A type of legend has grown up, books, films, and plays have seized upon it, and history has been grossly distorted as a result. It is easier to believe in a legend than to investigate hard facts. My concern here is not to do justice to Diaghileff, but to trace the development of ballet with accuracy.

V

From ignoring Diaghileff's role altogether to exaggerating it and ignoring that of many of his collaborators is an easy step. Diaghileff started his career under the strong influence of Benois and with a choreographer, Fokine, who was already formed. Before the start of the company, Fokine had produced *Nuits d'Égypte*, afterwards *Cleopatra*, *Chopiniana*, afterwards *Les Sylphides*, *Carnaval*, and, under the influence of Benois, *Le Pavillon d'Armide*. Diaghileff improved the detail of these works, had the Chopin and the Schumann re-orchestrated; but in this first phase his function was purely that of censor, propagandist, and impresario.

(a) Music

The characteristic of this first period of a year, 1909, is the use of adapted music. The Diaghileff Ballet begins to be a fully creative artistic force with the collaboration of Stravinsky the following year in *The Firebird*.

'Throughout the winter,' writes Stravinsky, 'I worked strenuously at my ballet, and that brought me into constant touch with Diaghileff and his collaborators. Fokine created the choreography of *The Firebird*, section by section, as the music was handed to him. I attended every rehearsal with the company, and after rehearsals Diaghileff, Nijinsky, and myself generally ended the day with a fine dinner, washed down with good claret.'

The significant phrases here are the *constant touch* and the *fine dinner*. It was on such informal occasions that Diaghileff worked, and the close association resulted in a whole series of ballets: *Petrouchka*, 1911; *Le Sacre du Printemps*, 1912; the ballets that made the name of Stravinsky and that interested the serious musicians in ballet, a hitherto despised art.

Stravinsky collaborated with Diaghileff till the end, not merely as a composer, but as minister of music to the cabinet. As soon as sufficient composers had become interested, no more ready-made music was used, though music was frequently adapted with marked success in such ballets as *Pulcinella*, *La Boutique Fantasque*, and *The Good-Humoured Ladies*.

To-day, there is no minister for music in the Russian Ballet cabinet, and the young composer is beginning to abandon ballet. One of the reasons for the artistic success of Sadler's Wells is that Constant Lambert, trained in the Diaghileff *milieu*, assumed that function.

(b) Décor

The décor of the Diaghileff Ballet was fully creative from the very start, under the guidance of Alexandre Benois. *The World of Art* had aimed at reforms in painting, and one of the reasons for the founding of the ballet was to give the new painting a platform. The artists concerned in the first decorative period from 1909 until the first year of the War were Russians: Benois, Bakst, Roerich, Korovin, Gontcharova, with the modernist Larionov as a bridge between the modern French painters and the Russians.

While Benois outlined the policy it was Bakst, with his glowing, exotic colours, who attracted the attention and who revolutionized the decorative art of the world. The change in decorative policy was brought about by two things – the accident of war that separated Benois and Diaghileff (Bakst remained a collaborator till the end of his life), and the quest of Diaghileff after novelty. He was always frightened of degenerating into a formula, eager to go in advance of the public taste. Even without the war such a change would have come about, and he was already interested in the work of Larionov, a Moscow painter who had come under the influence of Paris. The aesthetic of ballet swung from the new romanticism to the grotesque, from curves to angles. It was a natural reaction from the arabesque to the cold logic of a Picasso, and Picasso and his followers took the place of Benois. The easel artist replaced the professional theatre artist, and in his turn became a professional, the same evolution as in Russia itself. The essential thing to remember is the close collaboration throughout. Monte Carlo, where the ballet remained for some months in every year, was the G.H.Q. at which the artists in every medium met and exchanged ideas. To-day, without that close contact with the theatre, the easel artist is apt to remain a complete amateur. Throughout the life of the Diaghileff Ballet, when music and choreography declined, the décor remained on an exceptionally high level.

(c) Dancing

During its first years, until 1910, the Diaghileff Ballet remained a travelling branch of the Imperial Theatre, the dancers joining Diaghileff during their long vacation. There was only the difficulty of finding appropriate dates. When, after the *Giselle* scandal,[1] Nijinsky was dismissed from the Imperial Service, Diaghileff formed his own company and the artists were faced with a choice, but until the War of 1914 the supply of highly trained dancers was unfailing. After Pavlova's defection Diaghileff found in Karsavina an ideal ballerina: a woman of exceptional intelligence, in thorough

1. See *Diaghileff*, by Arnold L. Haskell.

sympathy with the new movement, and with a range of expression that made her available for every role. For a long time she continued a dual existence as a ballerina at St Petersburg, interpreting the classics, as the standard-bearer of the new ballet. Karsavina remains the ideal of the modern ballerina, with every attribute that I have outlined, and it is with her in mind that I have set my standards.

Closely associated with her was Vaslav Nijinsky. He became a legend, and it is difficult to write about legends. He was the first Russian male dancer to be seen in Western Europe; memory plays tricks, and how much greater he was than any other dancer since it is impossible to say. He was clearly a great instinctive artist, to whom technique was a servant.

Among the other artists of this great dancing period were Lydia Lopokova, later ballerina of the company, Lubov Tchernicheva, a strong dramatic actress fortunately still on the stage, and Adolf Bolm. But all were experienced in stagecraft and finished dancers of a type that belongs to the past. Among them was one exceptional English girl, Lydia Sokolova, whose musical knowledge and dramatic ability made her definitely one of them.

Diaghileff never at any time wished to alter either the type or the training of his dancers. His ideal was the pure classical ballerina. When war and revolution separated him from the great manufactory of ballerinas, he tried to reproduce the system abroad, engaging maestro Cecchetti for the classics and the intensive training of especially talented dancers.

Vera Nemtchinova became his first ballerina not trained in the Imperial schools, who had risen out of his own ranks. The fine Polish dancers, Idzikovski and Woizikovski, played an important role, stressing the invaluable work of Cecchetti in Warsaw. Many English dancers joined the company, among them Vera Savina, light, and of exceptional elevation, who made a great reputation, Ninette de Valois, Alicia Markova, and an Englishman, Anton Dolin, who became *premier danseur classique*.

Diaghileff engaged the strictly classical Olga Spessivtseva when he was able, Ludmila Schollar and Anatol Wilzak, magnificent *danseur noble*, and induced Vera Trefilova, the purest of all the classicists, to return to the stage, but almost imperceptibly a change was coming about. During his last three years the bulk of the work was entrusted to three highly talented but immature and not yet fully trained dancers: Alice Nikitina, Alexandra Danilova, and Serge Lifar, all of whom made names at a much later period. The programme could not be revealingly classical, and the modernist experiments did not assist in the training of the young dancers. It was a vicious circle. The period of the wonder children trained by the St Petersburg ballerina *émigrées* in Paris was still five years distant.

(d) Choreography

Until the 1914 War, with but a brief interregnum, Fokine was in charge of the choreography. It is interesting to note that out of thirteen works of his produced during that period eleven still survive, and *Les Sylphides*, *Carnaval*, *Prince Igor*, and *Petrouchka* are the most constantly given of all ballets. *Fokine is, beyond all question, the father of contemporary ballet, and his works are school pieces in the sense that they must be studied by everyone connected with ballet.*

The interregnum of 1912–13 was due to personal reasons, but the ballets of 1914, *Papillons* and *Joseph's Legend*, seem to show that Fokine was a little weary and inclined to repeat a success without success.

Nijinsky's ballets, with one exception, *l'Après-midi d'un Faune*, do not survive to-day. He was undoubtedly a greater dancer than choreographer; a man with something very definite to express, but without the means, the necessary musical knowledge, of expressing it. The constant contact with pure classicism seems to have inspired in him a revolt in which he wished to express strong primitive things in a jerky, angular fashion as far removed from the Fokine ballets as possible. The first attempt, *l'Après-midi d'un Faune*, caused a first-rate scandal, being attacked by the *Figaro* on moral grounds and defended by Rodin on aesthetic ones. This was followed by *Jeux*, a tennis ballet, which was a complete failure, and *Le Sacre du Printemps*, which provoked a still greater scandal. The Nijinsky legend must not blind us to facts. Stravinsky says of *Le Sacre du Printemps*: 'Nijinsky began by demanding such a fantastic number of rehearsals that it was physically impossible to give them to him. It will not be difficult to understand why he wanted so many, when I say that in trying to explain to him the construction of my work in general outline and in detail, I discovered that I should achieve nothing until I had taught him the very rudiments of music. ... When, in listening to music, he contemplated movements, it was always necessary to remind him that he must make them accord with the *tempo*, its divisions and values.'

The Nijinsky interregnum, however, was of value, even if the work was not. It shook the dancers from their composure and prevented the Russians from adopting a formula of success, and in similar fashion it shook the public and made them watch attentively. It is all too easy to take in alone the more obvious beauty of ballet, to watch it in a sort of trance and to ignore its character. The sudden shock of these scandals prevented that. The true enrichment of ballet and the movement away from neo-romanticism was brought about by Leonide Massine. Nijinsky paved the way.

Leonide Massine started his career as a soloist in 1914, and as choreographer in 1915. *He dominated the stage in both capacities for many years, one of the outstanding figures in the whole history of ballet.*

With Massine, the Diaghileff Ballet begins a new phase; it is truly the Diaghileff Ballet, while during the first few years the Diaghileff-Fokine Ballet would be a more accurate description.

When Nijinsky left the company, Diaghileff was faced with finding a successor to dance the role of the young Joseph in *Joseph's Legend*, an ambitious ballet commissioned from Richard Strauss. The work of a very young man in the Moscow school attracted his attention, and he engaged him. From the first, Massine showed unusual ability, taking advantage of the immense educational facilities given him. He devoured books, studied in museums, and listened to the conversation of artists. It was immediately obvious that this was to be no ordinary dancer. In accordance with the new tendencies of the ballet, Diaghileff entrusted a large part of his protégé's early artistic education to Larionov.

The first ballet, *The Midnight Sun*, a pagan Russian festival in a grotesque setting by Larionov, was produced in 1915 at the Opéra, Paris, for a war charity gala. It is still in the repertoire to-day, a slight work, but one that already reveals an extraordinary gift for the use of folk material. This was followed by some Spanish fragments, the education for *The Three-Cornered Hat*, and by a portion of what became *Contes Russes*. The influence of Larionov was still great. With his first full-length ballet, a masterpiece, *The Good-Humoured Ladies*, Massine became completely himself, producing ballet after ballet until he left in 1921. There could be no question of replacing him, no risk of his discovering a formula. He was infinitely varied, deeply interested in experiment. Following on Fokine's reforms and Nijinsky's unfulfilled ambitions, he greatly enriched the pattern of the dance, bringing to it the dances of Spain, the inspiration of Hogarth and Callot, the cubism of Picasso, and the spirit of the machine age. His invention is far from exhausted; he is the major figure in the contemporary ballet. At his worst he exaggerated movement in compositions that reminded one of the later Raphael, a phase that soon disappeared when he was no longer caught up in the modern movement and began to look back to classicism as a firm foundation. Massine left Diaghileff in 1921 for purely personal reasons, only to return later as a guest.

The fact of Massine leaving, as well as a sentimental memory of his youth, turned Diaghileff back to classicism. In an age of democracy he decided to present a lavish revival of the famous Maryinsky ballet: Tchaikovsky's *Sleeping Princess*. As usual, he prepared the ground with great care. The music was partly re-orchestrated by Stravinsky, who reassured the moderns that this was no retrograde step, that Tchaikovsky was the most characteristic of all Russian composers, and that they must not be deceived by the traditional Muscovite flavour absent in his music. The ballet was dressed and decorated by Léon Bakst and additional numbers from *Casse-Noisette* were incorporated into it. Diaghileff engaged the last of the classical ballerinas, Vera Trefilova and Olga Spessivtseva, for the role of Aurora, and greatly enriched his company. As a sentimental gesture characteristic of the man he engaged Carlotta Brianza, who had created the role of Aurora in the original production, to mime the wicked fairy Carabosse.

The result was the first truly classical Russian ballet on a grand scale that London had ever seen, and consequently the first opportunity to gain a real basic knowledge of ballet. For a quantity of reasons a work that would have enjoyed success to-day was a comparative failure.

Diaghileff was expected to provide surprises, but of a Left tendency, and in spite of his skilled propaganda he could not counterbalance a propaganda of the past. The man who had presented a cubist manifesto, *Parade*, was not expected to return to the aesthetics of his ancestors. His public was comparatively small, and not one that understood the finer points of ballet. The fashion was against him, and for once in his life he could not sway it. The work was very extravagantly produced, requiring a year's run to show any profit. A mechanical device went wrong on the first night and ruined an effective scene.

Diaghileff's lesson had its full effect only in retrospect. It undoubtedly set a standard of dancing.

The immediate reaction of this failure, which endangered the very existence of the company, was to make him turn to modernism once again. His new choreographer was Bronislava Nijinska, sister of Nijinsky, and a very remarkable dancer. Nijinska turned to choreography through necessity. She was teaching in Kiev with the ambition of forming dancers to interpret her brother's ballets. She saw that the orthodox curriculum was inadequate, and her first attempts at choreography consisted in exercises for her pupils. Through that departure she became the most personal of all choreographers, teaching the dancers first of all to think in terms of her work. For Diaghileff she produced one masterpiece, *Les Noces*, to Stravinsky's music, misunderstood in this country but warmly defended by H. G. Wells. *Les Noces* was a ballet of intricate mass movement that revealed the esoteric meaning of a Russian peasant marriage. Her other ballets were ingenious satires, works which by their outlook denied them permanence. *The Blue Train*, created for Anton Dolin, showed the use of acrobatic technique with a classical ballet plastique. It was a satire on the frequenters of the Riviera, handsome athletes, golf and tennis champions, and bathers. *Les Biches*, with music by Poulenc and admirable interpretative scenery by Marie Laurencin, was a vicious commentary on a group of modern nymphs, ladies of pleasure, and their reactions when three handsome athletes entered their establishment. It was disguised in England under the grossly misleading title of *The House Party*.

Nijinska has been unfortunate in her ballets. The Diaghileff material denied them the permanence that their choreography demanded. Later, she did magnificent work for Ida Rubinstein with *Bolero*, *La Valse*, *La Bienaimée*, *Les Noces de Psyché et de l'Amour*, seen only for a few weeks. For her own very short-lived company she produced *Les Comédiens Jaloux*, *Beethoven Variations*, and *Hamlet*. All these works deserved a permanent company to present them. Her influence on dancing, however, has been profound. Lifar, Lichine, Dolin, Shabelevsky, Verchinina, Morosova, Ashton, and others all owe an immense debt to her training.

When she left Diaghileff her place was taken by Georges Balanchine, who came to him more formed than either Massine or Nijinska. Balanchine, a pupil of the Imperial schools and a fine musician, had begun to emerge during the Revolution, but his work was considered too artistically revolutionary for Russia and he left with a small group of dancers. His ballets for Diaghileff came during a bad period, and, though they caused a sensation, the public had dwindled to a small and rather precious clique. The best known were *La Chatte*, *The Gods go a-begging*, *Barabau*, *Apollon Musagètes*, and *Le Fils Prodigue*, not one of which survives. They were ingenious and intensely personal distortions of classicism that promptly dated as none of the earlier Diaghileff ballets had done.

The last choreographer of the company was Serge Lifar. In Stravinsky's *Le Renard*, under the guidance of Larionov, master of the grotesque, he tried the interesting experiment of presenting movement done by both dancers and acrobats, but he lacked the necessary experience to get the most out of it.

This long experimental phase produced many interesting

results, but on the whole it was based on the sensationalism that Diaghileff had learned from the scandals of the Nijinsky régime. In much of the work Diaghileff himself did not believe. He was frightened of old age and of being superseded, and was indulging in a mad chase after youth. These experiments would eventually have killed ballet. They ended just in time, and there is evidence that had Diaghileff lived he himself would have turned his back on them. His last performance ended with a magnificent revival of *The Swan Lake*, in which Spessivtseva, classical ballerina *par excellence*, shone.

The company held in it the seeds of the future. Lifar went as choreographer and *premier danseur* to the original home of ballet – the Opéra, Paris, and has dominated the dance there ever since. Tcherkas went to the Opéra Comique. Balanchine and Grigorieff were among the founders of the de Basil Company. Ninette de Valois founded the Vic-Wells Ballet, and Markova and Dolin were its first stars. Massine is still the biggest figure in ballet to-day. The company as an entity died with its great founder, but so living was his inspiration that fragments of it took root all over the world, and to-day dominate the whole movement. Bolm is settled in Chicago, Balanchine founded the American Ballet in New York, Nijinska worked in Buenos Aires, Nemtchinova and Zvereff went to Kovno. Everywhere the name of Diaghileff lives on.

He died in Venice in 1929, and his mortal remains lie buried there.

II. ANNA PAVLOVA

An exception to the rule

I

Outside Russia Anna Pavlova was greatly misunderstood by the very people who should best have appreciated her art. Were she to return today she would gain a new and far more critical audience.

Such a statement about an artist whose name is to this day synonymous with dancing may seem a paradox. It is not.

Pavlova was seen and admired the world over, but largely by people who were not deeply interested in the art of ballet, who would flock to the Winter Garden Pavilion to see Kreisler one week, Harry Lauder the next, and Pavlova the next. They went into raptures at her daintiness, marvelled at the fact that she could dance on the points of her toes. They most certainly missed the essentials of her art, a fact that worried her in spite of her success. One very definite effect upon those audiences the world over, apart from a memory of beauty to light up a drab existence, was to determine them to have their daughters taught dancing. Schools sprang up like mushrooms in her wake. When I have asked countless dancers all over the world what made them start, the answer is more often than not: 'Mother saw Pavlova', or 'I saw Pavlova'. There has never been so great a propagandist force for the art of dancing: England, the Dominions, the Colonies, America, Mexico, South America, Java, China, Japan, all saw and marvelled.

The small clique of people who really enjoyed ballet, who could discuss it in an amazing technical jargon, stood aloof. To them ballet meant one thing alone: the surprises in music, décor, and choreography brought them yearly by Diaghileff. That and that alone meant ballet. They had very little conception of dancing itself as a great interpretative art.

When I first met Pavlova she said to me: 'Are you on my side or Diaghileff's?' At the time the remark seemed to me unnecessary, and I could not grasp its significance. It was many years before I understood it clearly, after both Pavlova and Diaghileff were dead. There were sides and there should not have been; a proper understanding of the art, such as that of the great critic André Levinson, consisted of a balance between the two. Both Pavlova and Diaghileff were the architects of contemporary ballet. Had one of them alone been responsible the result would have been a leaning tower of Pisa; certainly a good deal less stable, ready to be destroyed by the first gale of criticism.

Pavlova and Diaghileff set out on the journey together. Pavlova was one of Diaghileff's main inspirations. He was to go to Paris to show this amazing product of Russian Ballet.

Diaghileff held modern views; we have seen the effect of the reaction on his group of what was being produced at the Maryinsky. Pavlova also was a rebel, a romantic who wished to escape from the pure virtuosity of classicism.

Pavlova was *The Dying Swan*, and Fokine's one-person ballet was truly a manifesto of the new choreographic outlook, difficult as such a conception may appear to us to-day.

Let us take the Swan Princess of *The Swan Lake* and Fokine's creation. In the first the Swan was undisguisedly a ballerina who used the story to reveal her gifts as a dancer. If she was an outstanding personality and a dramatic actress as well, so much the better. She could make it more interesting than it actually was. *The Dying Swan* was never an excuse for pyrotechnics. In technique it was absurdly simple – any pupil could master the steps in a short time; but the steps were only the beginning, the means to an end, and the end was to interpret the atmosphere of the music and to convey a tragedy. *The Dying Swan* showed the death of an ephemeral creature and not the prowess of a ballerina. As such, it was the manifesto of Fokine's new romanticism. At the start Pavlova's path, Fokine's path, and Diaghileff's path were identical.

II

Anna Pavlova was born in St Petersburg, a weak and premature child, on January 31st, 1882. She was not expected to live. She was removed to Ligova, in the country outside the city, and the air soon proved beneficial. Her love of the country, her direct contact with nature, were to colour her entire artistic outlook, and many of her best-known dances are an interpretation of nature: *The Dragonfly*, *The Californian Poppy*, *Autumn Leaves*.

As a holiday treat she was taken to see a matinée of *The Sleeping Princess*, as so many children were to be taken to see her and with the same result. From that moment her mind was made up. Her mother took her to the Imperial schools, but to her bitter disappointment she was too young. Pupils were not received before the age of ten (a warning to the impatient parent of to-day), and she still had two more years to wait. During those two years her resolve grew still stronger.

When the time came, she had to face a dreaded test. There were about a hundred candidates, with only seven or eight vacancies, and a formidable jury of directors and dancers, past and present. Health was an essential and Pavlova was still frail. It speaks well for the discernment of the judges that she was among those selected. The course took seven years, and consisted not only of dancing but of an excellent general and artistic education. She was taught by A. Oblakov, the former ballerina Vasem, and an outstanding actor-dancer, Paul Gerdt, pupil of Johannsen. Gerdt took an enormous interest in his unusual pupil, teaching her in such a way as to turn her frailty into an asset. She finished her schooling at the age of seventeen with the high grade of 'first dancer'.

The later Valerian Svetloff, an enlightened critic, describes her début.

'I found myself in a cosy little corner, in the lighted, warm green realm of the dryads. This little corner was the Mikhailovsky Theatre and the dryads proved to be unreal, for they were represented by ordinary pupils of the theatrical school ...

'The jury sat in the front row, putting down marks to the dryads. This alone somewhat destroyed the illusion. ...

'It was on this evening that for the first time the public saw the pupil, Pavlova, and it was on this evening that for the first time she attracted the attention of everybody. ... With childish ingenuousness she acted a *scène de coquetterie* with a young peasant and with playful wantonness danced with the imaginary dryads. All this was youthfully gay and pretty, and nothing more need be said, except that the play of the child's features in the scene with the peasant was already full

of expression, and one had the feeling that here was something individual, something that was not learnt by rote at school. But in the solo variation from *The Vestal Virgin* one already felt something more, something that made it possible for one, without posing as a prophet, to foresee in the youthful dancer a future great artist.'

Valerian Svetloff, my master as a critic, followed this career step by step, outliving Pavlova by several years. May he rest in a heaven where Taglioni and his own beloved Pavlova for ever dance.

Pavlova continued for some time as a pupil, when already on the stage, learning in Johannsen's perfection classes. But one generation separated Johannsen from Vestris. Pavlova was of the real aristocracy of ballet.

Within a few years she had made an immense reputation, sealing it with her interpretation of *Giselle*. Her ethereal qualities, in striking contrast to the more robust strength of her contemporaries, awoke memories of Taglioni and suggested a new romanticism. In 1905 she became a pupil of Cecchetti, adding something of Italian strength and precision to her frail grace. The dancer, unlike any other artist, is always a pupil even at the very height of her fame, and Cecchetti continued to be her master for many years. One of the greatest differences between the ballerina of yesterday and of to-day was the realization that learning is never finished. The ballerina of to-day, once famous, has not the opportunity to increase her knowledge, even when she has the desire. Pavlova may have ruled her own company as a complete autocrat, but there was always someone to whom she was the pupil in need of guidance and correction.

Pavlova's first journey abroad was to Riga in 1908, with a small company, and the following year she visited Scandinavia and Germany. It was the beginning of her triumphal campaign.

III

Her successes abroad played their part in deciding Diaghileff to undertake his adventure. Fokine, the chosen choreographer of the new movement, had found in Pavlova a true inspiration. 'She is the greatest ballerina in the world, excelling both in classicism and in character. Like a Taglioni she doesn't dance, but floats; of her, also, one might say that she could walk over a cornfield without bending an ear.'

So spoke Diaghileff to Gabriel Astruc one evening at Paillard's when the question of bringing Russian Ballet to Paris first arose. And Pavlova came to Paris to dance with the Diaghileff Ballet. Jean Louis Vaudoyer wrote of her: 'Mademoiselle Pavlova is to dancing what a Racine is to poetry, a

Poussin to painting, a Gluck to music.' But, in spite of this praise from an exceptionally understanding critic, Pavlova was overshadowed in the press by Nijinsky in *Les Sylphides* and Ida Rubinstein in *Cleopatra*. To-day, this seems difficult to understand. But in Paris in 1909 a male dancer was a complete novelty, and also Diaghileff was personally interested in launching his protégé. The 'Biblical Rubinstein', who posed rather than danced and who was the centrepiece of a sensational scene, being unwrapped from her mummy clothes to appear in all her striking beauty, represented the exotic element expected from the Russians. Whatever the cause, this distribution of praise altered the career of Pavlova and with it the history of ballet. The first poster of the Russian Ballet bore her portrait, she was a part, a large part, of the inspiration, but she left at the end of the first season.

This departure left behind a permanent trace of bitterness, and Diaghileff was never fair to Pavlova, going out of his way to extol an obviously inferior ballerina, comparatively speaking, at her expense. Pavlova clearly remained his ideal, hence the note of hostility when he said: 'Pavlova was never really interested in art as such. The only thing that mattered to her was virtuosity, and she is a virtuoso without equal. When first I wanted her to do Stravinsky's *The Firebird*, especially designed for her, she declared that she wouldn't dance to such horrible music.'

This estimate of Pavlova as primarily a virtuoso is patently ridiculous. She was never a virtuoso and, judged by such standards, there were and are many far greater than she. She revolted against virtuosity in the same way as Fokine and Diaghileff himself had done. She was greatly interested in art, only her viewpoint began to differ, partly no doubt through reaction against Diaghileff.

She saw the art of ballet menaced by modern tendencies and rallied to its defence. The phrase: 'Are you on my side or

Diaghileff's?' was for her full of meaning, especially spoken at a time when he was on the extreme Left and she, as if to balance him, on the extreme Right. She danced for him once again as a guest artist during the Coronation season in 1911. The rest of her career consists of voyages and triumphs right up to the day of her death.

Diaghileff's aesthetic was a personal one, but expressed through the medium of others; consequently it was by its very nature more objective. Pavlova's was expressed through her own mind and body. She was surrounded by a company, but that company was a background and her whole balletic conception was subjective, whether this was her conscious aim or not. In fact, it was not, for she thought of ballet in the wider sense, even though the word was always spelt Pavlova.

Early in her travels the Russian and Polish members in her company came to blows, and she found it impossible to manage them. From this moment she deliberately filled her company with English dancers. Their docility was the first point in their favour. Later, their aptitude for the dance became more apparent. During her lifetime the Pavlova company was of no importance; when she died it became of outstanding importance. She had trained a whole generation. If they did not make a name as individuals, they became teachers and missionaries. The discipline she had given them and the type of girl that she selected proved that ballet was a possible career for the carefully brought up 'daughters of gentlemen', and not an excuse for a life of frivolity. From both sides of the stage Pavlova's value as a propagandist cannot be overestimated, and that propaganda continues as well as the inspiration of her art. What type of artist was she? What did she express and how does she fit into the history of ballet?

IV

It is best to begin with a physical portrait. I have already mentioned her fragility; it was only in appearance when she began her career, for she enjoyed robust health until the day of her untimely death. Physically, she was remarkable, with long, perfectly proportioned arms that accentuated the large movements so characteristic of the Russian school; exceptionally well-modelled legs showing none of the bulging, over-developed muscle so characteristic of many dancers; strong slender ankles, and a highly developed instep as strong as steel. Her face was not beautiful in a conventional sense; it was interesting and it was the perfect instrument for her art. She could assume beauty at will: the wild beauty of the Bacchante, the exotic beauty of the gipsy, or the sweet pretti-ness of the girl in such a fragment as *Noël*. When she was no longer young and her face in repose betrayed some of the ravages of an exceptionally hard life, it would on the stage appear still young and almost girlish; not the result of make-up – I watched her often enough from the wings – but of artistry. There was very little difference between the young Pavlova and the Pavlova of the last few years. The head was beautifully placed on the shoulders. She moved with a natural grace, which teaching had accentuated, and many of her dances were dances of grace rather than show pieces.

Her range was a wide one, combining both Taglioni and Elssler; but she excelled in the portrayal of the pathetic, of some ephemeral being that came to life and then withered and died all on a summer's day.

Much has been written of her love of birds and flowers. Such topics are a joy to the press agent, but the birds are all too often caged and the flowers wired. In the case of Pavlova this close observation of nature and the identification of herself with nature has a very definite meaning. Her Swan, Dragonfly, and Poppy were not portraits in the exact sense of the word, but they were translations that could have been made only by someone who really felt in complete harmony with nature. What struck me the most about Pavlova was not just the fact that her dancing seemed entirely spontaneous, but that it seemed a natural phenomenon, like the ripple of a pond, the opening of a flower, or the leaves being whisked and whirled by the wind. Such imaginative descriptions may seem extravagant, especially in the English language, and they are used by a critic who usually mistrusts them profoundly, but they represent the only manner in which one can convey something of the impression created by Pavlova. It is, perhaps, because of this gift of appearing natural that one was inclined to take her for granted and only to begin to analyse her after her death.

It is always said that she rose above her material by what Benois has aptly termed 'a theatrical miracle', that she danced the dances of every day as no one had ever done, and this is true. When she died a number of roles died with her. She was creative, for she had created these roles out of almost nothing; and even a great conception like *The Dying Swan* has become an impossibility without her.

But those phrases are also used as a reproach and must be examined from that point of view. The dancer is a part of a complicated organism, and her personality and artistry must not be allowed to become the sole *raison d'être* of ballet. There is no doubt that *Les Sylphides* was more worthy of her gifts than the indifferent *Chopiniana* in which she danced; that *The Firebird* is a living work of art where *Don Quixote* was killed at birth by its wretched music; that *The Fairy Doll* has no artistic justification. This is admitted, the whole trend of this book has been to explain and insist upon such facts. The Pavlova of a great work, *Giselle*, was the greatest Pavlova of all. While we accept this, we cannot blame Pavlova herself. There was and is no machinery into which she could be fitted. She had left the Maryinsky far behind, and after the first few years the atmosphere of the Diaghileff Ballet was a hostile one. We cannot see Pavlova even in such great works as *La Boutique Fantasque* or *The Good-Humoured Ladies*. She was an organization on her own as well as an individual; there were the Maryinsky, Diaghileff, and Pavlova. That is the important point to remember. Maryinsky and Diaghileff could continue, but Pavlova was as ephemeral as the beings she so truly interpreted. The machinery that grew up around her was, by its very nature, both temporary and a compromise. If we do not remember her, it will not bear critical examination. There was nothing more pathetic than the few performances of the Pavlova Ballet without Pavlova. This machinery, however, was worthily conceived. She could as a concert dancer have attracted the masses. People, in any case, came to see *The Dying Swan* rather than anything else. It is a tribute to her conscience as an artist that she realized that only in a large *ensemble* could she really shine. There is no truth in the supposition that jealousy prevented her from appearing with other great artists. She may or may not have been jealous, but she outshone her generation and had nothing to fear. She shone alone against a drab but worthy background, because she was an exception to every rule and it is impossible to fit a lasting framework round an exception.

Her importance in the history of ballet and as one of the founders of the contemporary movement lies in the fact that she proved to the world that the ballet dancer could be a completely expressive artist, the equal of a Duse, a Bernhardt, or a Chaliapine. She stands as an ideal and an inspiration, and her value as an influence lives on after her.

The phrase 'Pavlova as an ideal and an inspiration' must not be misunderstood, as it so often is when people ignorantly talk of 'a second Pavlova'. Had Pavlova been a second Taglioni she would never have made an impression. She was the first and only Pavlova. There may be equally great dancers in the future, not reflections of Pavlova, but fresh personalities.

The machinery that produced a Pavlova has been broken by economic conditions, but true genius will find a way.

The only manner in which to understand Pavlova as an ideal is to understand her attitude towards her art and the true extent of her accomplishment. She started with lavish natural gifts and she transformed them into conscious artistry, ceaselessly learning and perfecting what she had been given.

III. COLONEL V. DE BASIL

Colonel Vassili de Basil has played an immense role in the popularization of ballet all over the world, and while he brought nothing new to the art he must occupy an important position in any history of ballet.

De Basil was not a theatre man by profession. He was a Colonel of Cossacks, a soldier with a distinguished war record. After the Russian Revolution he started a theatrical and concert agency, and a small troupe of dancers that was more or less a family affair. In 1931, in partnership with Prince Tseretelli, he became director of a Russian opera company that came to the Lyceum with Chaliapine as its star. It was during this season with its occasional evening of ballet that de Basil began to plan the formation of a company that would succeed that of Diaghileff.

His task was a formidable one. The ballet public was re-

stricted, and was convinced that no one could succeed Diaghileff. The dancers were scattered all over the world, and would
not easily subject themselves to the discipline of a newcomer,
especially one without experience and without capital. But
de Basil's ambition was boundless, and he started with a
trump card, an association with a highly cultivated Frenchman, René Blum at Monte Carlo, the cradle of *ballet russe*.
De Basil formed his company with very great skill. He called
on the experienced Balanchine, Massine, Grigorieff, Tchernicheva, Woizikovsky, and Danilova, thus assuring himself
the true succession, and he recruited some sensational children,
among them Baronova, Toumanova, Riabouchinska, Verchinina, and Lichine.

In 1932 he opened at Monte Carlo, and the following year, on
July 4th, at the Alhambra, London. It was to have been a three
weeks' season; it lasted five months, gaining a reprieve for the
famous music-hall doomed to be replaced by a super-colossal
cinema. On December 17th of that year he began the first of
his American tours at the St James' Theatre, New York.

And everywhere it was the same – the era of balletomania
had begun, the baby ballerinas attracted the attention of a
larger public than ballet had ever known.

These thirteen-year-olds differed considerably from the
previous generations of Russian dancers. Suffering had given
them a precocity unknown to their carefully cloistered elders.
It had given them a close contact with humanity. Also, compared to their predecessors, their training was perfunctory,
but two factors gave them exceptional technical facility.

Teaching had made extraordinary progress, and they were
being taught by the most experienced dancers of their day;
also the modern girl is physically stronger and more of a
natural athlete than the corseted girl of pre-war days. These
children were able to perform feats of virtuosity that had
rarely been attempted before.

The *fouetté* is a case in point. More than anything else it made the popularity of the new ballet. The public is always over-susceptible to virtuosity. The *fouetté* was first launched, if not invented, by the Italian, Pierrina Legnani. In the third act of *The Swan Lake* her series of thirty-two caused a sensation, eager balletomanes counting aloud, as if it had been an exhibition of athletics, which in many respects it was. The sensitive critic found it out of place in this romantic ballet, though, in fact, there was a slender dramatic justification, since the bewitched girl is meant to dazzle the Prince by her brilliance. For a long time no Russian could emulate Legnani, until finally Kchesinska found out the secret, amidst national rejoicing. Even then it was by no means universal, neither Pavlova nor Karsavina adopting it. This rare trick of the multiple *fouetté*, not properly in the dancer's repertoire, became a commonplace to the young dancers of the emigration. They could perform thirty-two, sixty-four, and more, if necessary, and they did it with ease and precision. It was now no more a trick but a part of the current language of dancing, and as such, the choreographer could use it expressively to tell his story and not to surprise the audience. We have in a previous chapter seen the slender division between dancing and acrobatics.[1] The first ballets in the de Basil repertory all contained *fouettés*, and the *fouettés* entranced the audience, gave the critics something to discuss, and launched thirteen-year-old Toumanova and Baronova as stars. The fact that they had other merits speedily dawned on the public. They attracted immediate attention by their technique, they retained it through their artistic instinct. It was too early to discuss conscious artistry.

De Basil banked everything upon the success of three unknown children: Toumanova, Baronova, and Riabouchinska. He was careful to give them the support of experienced

1. See page 43.

artists, but the onus of the performance fell on them, Danilova only joining the company later, and with them began the world-wide popularity of ballet. In Diaghileff's day ballet as a whole rather than individual dancers had attracted the attention; with de Basil it was the opposite. The young dancers became stars, the public went to see them, and remained to enjoy the art.

The first season's programmes were noteworthy; they seemed to be carrying on the Diaghileff tradition with French art as the inspiration. Balanchine created *Concurrence* with Auric and Derain, *Cotillon* with Bérard to the music of Chabrier, and Massine was the choreographer of *Jeux d'Enfants* with Mirò to the music of Bizet, and revived the still running *Beau Danube* to the most perfect cast: Massine himself as the Hussar, Danilova as the Street Dancer, Riabouchinska as the young girl and Baronova as the Midinette. These first performances will be remembered by all who saw them; they were to be the Indian summer of *ballet russe*. But the big sensation and the controversy – and here again we were brought back to a typical Diaghileff situation – was caused by the symphonic ballets, *Les Présages* to Tchaikovsky's fifth symphony, *Choreartium* to Brahms' fourth, and *La Symphonie Fantastique* of Berlioz, all with choreography by Massine. For the most part the balletomanes praised and the music critics condemned, though their doyen, Ernest Newman, came out strongly in the ballets' favour. They were remarkably interpreted by the full strength of the company. Verchinina as Action, Baronova and Lichine as Passion, and Riabouchinska as Folly in *Les Présages* gave unforgettable performances. These works have played a major role in the history of the art, not as artistic innovations but from the point of view of setting an example, especially as it indicated a line of least resistance, the use of non-copyright and already recorded music popular with audiences. To-day the symphonies and concertos are daily butchered to make a balletomane's holiday. Everything, of course, depends on the choreographer and the choice of work; even Massine failed when confronted with Beethoven.

I will summarize the arguments pro and con without myself taking a determined stand on either side, or, perhaps, taking yet a third position; not that I have ever believed in sitting on the fence, but because the evidence here seems to warrant it.

The musical purists maintain, and rightly so, that a symphony is a complete and independent work of art; consequently that anything that is added to it is completely superfluous; that it does not lend itself either to amplification or to illustration. In 1909 the musical purists made the same objection against *Les Sylphides*, reinforced by the fact that Chopin's music had to be orchestrated. While *Les Sylphides* and *Carnaval* are the beginnings of using music for ballet written for another purpose, one must not drive the comparison too far. No one claims that their music is *absolute* in the same sense as the symphonies, and the choreographer has some powers of selection denied him in a continuous forty-five minute composition. I merely mention this early objection to show that the musical purist tends to think in terms of the concert-hall rather than of theatrical effectiveness. The ballet is essentially theatre, and good theatre can under certain circumstances excuse what is bad taste on paper. The musical purist is invariably right on paper. The main question in the case of the symphonies is whether the circumstances excuse the use of this particular music.

The ballet die-hard, frequently more emotional than thoughtful, replies with a number of arguments. His main contention is that the choreographer does not seek either to amplify or illustrate this absolute music, but to create movement that is parallel in thought. Also, he goes on to say that any music that inspires a muscular reaction is suitable for dancing, and that this music very clearly does or it would not be danced to at all. He finally begs the purist to stay away and let him enjoy his ballet symphony in peace, even if there are grave doubts about its artistic taste.

My own reaction is somewhere between the two. I believe that the symphony by its nature is unsuited to ballet and that the almost complete success of three symphonic ballets proves nothing, especially since two of them are not typical, and the one that is is the weakest. The ballet symphony can never develop into a school. These particular ballets were isolated experiments in which Massine succeeded to an astonishing degree in creating a parallelism of movement and sound. It is in the more architectural grouping, beautiful in itself, that one finds the impossibility of any parallelism. The music does not allow the dancers to leave the groups that have been assumed, and the breakaway is clumsy and suddenly separates motion from music. This was especially noticeable in the first part of Berlioz' *Symphonie Fantastique*. Both *Les Présages* (Tchaikovsky's 5th Symphony) and Berlioz' *Symphonie Fantastique* lend themselves to a story; in the second part of the Berlioz Massine devised some of the noblest choreography of our age; in the second part of the Tchaikovsky some of the most moving and theatrically effective. It is in the Brahms that the choice of music was the least happy. For the first of many visits the plastically-minded, as opposed to the musically-minded, took in only the magnificent moving frescoes; it was with repeated visits that the difference between music and movement became noticeable and finally jarred in such places as the *fouettés* and the *tours-en-l'air* of the final tableau.

Such typical classroom virtuosity can never parallel the musical thought, which is lost when the music degenerates into a rhythmic accompaniment. These works are outstanding examples of great choreography, yet I would hesitate before calling them great ballets in the sense that *Petrouchka* is so unquestionably a great ballet. In the same way to-day I would rate Petit's *Le Loup* far higher than his great dramatic ballet *Carmen* because *Le Loup* with its specially composed score has greater completeness. These symphonic ballets lack that element of completeness. To use a colloquialism, 'Massine got away with it'. Whether he or anyone else will do so again is another matter. The failure of the Beethoven 7th Symphony, apart from the noble second movement, shows that. They would be ill-advised to try.

In addition to the creations, de Basil revived many Diaghileff ballets, giving to a new generation the opportunity of seeing *The Polovsian Dances from Prince Igor, Schéhérazade, Thamar, Le Tricorne, La Boutique Fantasque* and, of course, *Les Sylphides* and *Carnaval.*

Unfortunately the promise of the first seasons could not be maintained, partly through economic pressure, partly through faulty planning. The first and greatest mistake was to part from Monte Carlo and from the highly cultured René Blum and his circle of French artists. The ballet was successful and, like the unfortunate *Wilis*, it literally danced itself to death. Yearly from 1934 to 1939 it came to Covent Garden, leaving to do its annual tour of over a hundred American cities.

There was no time to create, to repair, or to rehearse. The dancers lived in a barrage of publicity, in which, unfortunately, they believed. Soon the inevitable quarrels led to a split; René Blum[1] started a new Monte Carlo company, the lawyers enriched themselves, and the dancers ran from one side to the other. De Basil was left with a popular repertoire that was progressively less well danced.

But de Basil's work was done; through him America discovered that ballet was not merely a girl and music diversion for the tired business-man. The 'modern dance' had never

1. René Blum was murdered in a German assassination camp during the occupation of France.

really attracted large audiences. Now through Agnes de Mille and others it was to influence ballet. Through de Basil Australia learnt to dance and to form its own company, led by a former de Basil dancer, Edouard Borovansky. And throughout the war years de Basil travelled in South America, bringing ballet to cities that had seen no dancer since Pavlova.

After the war de Basil tried to reassemble a new company for New York and London. It was a failure, the old magic had vanished. Both cities had companies of their own that had reached a high standard and, however good the repertoire, they were used to watching a team and not a hastily assembled group of dancers.

De Basil struggled to the end. He died suddenly, in Paris in 1952, while just about to launch yet another company.

Every balletomane owes him a vast debt of gratitude. He provided the bridge between the Diaghileff era and the present day of national companies. He created a world public, and he stimulated the newcomers; he filled the dancing schools. He never made a penny for himself, but he left us all rich; not only in memories.

CHAPTER SIX

The Architects of Contemporary Ballet

I. NINETTE DE VALOIS

EDRIS STANNUS, an Irish dancer who assumed the name of a line of French kings, much to Diaghileff's disgust – he always insisted on spelling it Devalois – is the only personality with a double claim to belong to this section of our study. As an animator of the Diaghileff-de Basil type, she has founded a truly national ballet that is important enough to be considered internationally; as a choreographer she is a pioneer in England, as well as one of the two major women choreographers in the history of the art. She has still a third claim, as a teacher who has discovered and launched two entire companies.

She started in the worst manner possible, as a child prodigy at a time when child prodigies and English (Irish) dancers were by no means the fashion. It was still necessary to adopt a change of name. De Valois herself *a changé tout cela*. She even survived such enthusiastic criticism as 'that charming child genius' and 'the child is a poem', tributes I have preserved in my collection of curiosities. De Valois was an admirable dancer with a fine technique and an intelligence that informed all her work. But it is not as a dancer that she gains her outstanding position in the history of ballet.

After a variety of engagements she joined the Diaghileff company in 1924 as a small *soliste*, her finest work being the 'finger variation' in *Aurora's Wedding*. She used her time there to study methods of teaching and production, a child among them taking notes; dancing was never an end in itself. Two years later she left the company, dissatisfied with the ballet aesthetic of the day. She founded a school of her own with what seemed at the time the pompous and ambitious title of the Academy of Choreographic Art. This she used as a headquarters, travelling to Dublin to produce for the Abbey Theatre and to Cambridge for the Festival Theatre. Her work in these theatres, in addition to her experience of pure ballet, decided her future bent. Working with actors unused to movement in the dancing sense, she was compelled to use theatrical production that would be effective. She gained at this time a rare conception of the relation between ballet and theatre. Fokine, a great producer quite apart from his choreography, was also trained in the dramatic schools. It is characteristic of de Valois that on the very first occasion that she met Robert Helpmann she said to him: 'Something can be done with that face,' thinking in a direction alien to the ordinary choreographer.

There seemed to be something a little smug and ridiculous about this young dancer who disapproved of the direction that the greatest of all companies was taking, and who formed her own Academy. It must have required an almost overpowering self-confidence. To have paused to examine the situation even for an instant would have meant failure. Thousands of dancers must have envied her the excellent position in the Russian Ballet, and she gave it up simply to follow a line of her own at a time when it was quite impossible for anyone but Diaghileff to gain a hearing. This stubborn determination against what seems at the time to be common sense is characteristic of Ninette de Valois.

The first works that she produced did not seem to justify her decision, even when one made due allowance for the material available. They showed the urgent desire to express something strong, they were well produced, but they were dull because she was so obviously in earnest and almost ridiculously young.

A critic who did not divine anything more than worthy

determination at the time of *Rout*, a naïve mixture of Central Europe and Celtic Twilight, can scarcely blame himself for a lack of perspicacity. There were violent extremes in de Valois' artistic conceptions, between brutal masculine strength and finicky, fluttering, feminine weakness. The one quality that characterized her work was musical conscientiousness, amounting at times to pedantry. She has a knowledge of musical construction that is rare in anyone.

Until the formation of the Camargo Society, 1930, she had proved nothing positive. I would even say, from my own observations and from the talk of dancers, that as a producer she was then inclined to drill all the personality out of her cast, counting the music till mathematics had driven the atmosphere away.

The first revelations were the Camargo productions, *Job* and *La Création du Monde*. Here were big conceptions treated in the grand manner. One hesitated to call them ballets, rather grudgingly even, but one began to look at de Valois in a new light, to see that she was neither smug nor cantankerous, but someone with a great deal to express and the necessary craft with which to express it. A pretty *Cephalus and Procris* and an intolerably dull *Origin of Design* seemed to confirm the original impression that she was not truly a choreographer. Their craft was competent, but they never came to life; certainly they never even gave a hint of the personality of their creator.

The Camargo Society undoubtedly had a marked effect on Ninette de Valois apart from the opportunity it gave her. It turned the earnest young rebel into someone who could value and understand the full meaning of collaboration. It brought her into contact with others who were trying to create, curbed some of her intolerance, turning it into a creative channel.

When Lilian Baylis summoned Ninette de Valois to work

at the Old Vic, two women admirably calculated to understand one another met. Lilian Baylis had a one-track mind, the success of her theatre; de Valois also, the success of her ballet; and, since the tracks led in the same direction, the force was irresistible. The essence of Lilian Baylis' success was a knowledge of human nature and the bigness of character to put implicit faith in anyone in whom she had learned to believe. And she believed in de Valois enough to let the handful of girls composing the opera ballets grow into a permanent ballet company. Looked at in cold blood by someone who knows the full difficulties, both women seemed insane.

De Valois must undoubtedly have made a considerable sacrifice to undertake what seemed an incredibly uphill task. Her school was a commercial success and she was beginning to make a name. Unhesitatingly she threw all her resources into the new enterprise and closed the school, accompanied by her pupils and a charming dancer, Ursula Moreton, as assistant. The company in the beginning was merely an embellishment to the opera, and attracted very little attention. One had to be a blind patriot to talk of British Ballet. Lilian Baylis was willing to gamble on its success, de Valois was building deliberately and systematically. The Wells then engaged Alicia Markova (and, at times, Anton Dolin) as a guest artist. Markova had a very considerable public who learnt the way to Rosebery Avenue, and the help that she gave the young enterprise was invaluable, though artistically, at the time, the partnership did not show great results. Markova was the solitary star, the Wells company a background devoid of personality. The ballets were built round Markova, the classics were revived for her, and it was obviously impossible to give to any of the young dancers roles in which she was shining. In any case, they were not yet ready. The ease of her position, the lack of any cause for apprehension that it might be menaced, would not have benefited Markova in the long run. With considerable foresight she decided to leave. The general opinion was that her absence would kill the Sadler's Wells Ballet, and there were talks of engaging another ballerina. Wisely this was not done. It would have strangled the enterprise.

Then Ninette de Valois revealed herself, within a few weeks, not only as a choreographer – after *The Rake's Progress* we were beginning to realize her strength – but as an animator, organizer, teacher. The company suddenly came into being from one week to another, almost dramatically. The outsider could have no perception of the intensive preparation that had been going on. The opportunity arose and the company was ready; young, a trifle raw, but a genuine personality, where before it had been a group of schoolgirls and boys. The seasons that followed this birth of the company – for the company was born the very moment it could rely on the dancers it had itself formed – proved a striking testimony to the leadership of de Valois. Progress was normal, that was the keynote of the work. If a dancer showed promise she developed gradually, not shining one week and a total eclipse the next. The erratic brilliance of the young Russians had made us forget the meaning of normal progress.

De Valois has discovered and developed an altogether extraordinary amount of talent. I do not believe that it is the result of flair, so much as knowledge. She has the ability to see what the result must be, if such and such a course of conduct is followed in the case of such and such a dancer. She is not misled by early success or failure; she has her own very positive ideas about talent that are frequently in open contradiction to those around her, and time and time again she has been right, right because she knows and not by intuition. She does not wait for the talent to declare itself, but waits for the right moment and then openly intervenes. The most extraordinary development had been the progress from the rather dry pedagogue to the truly creative teacher, a thing difficult to account for, unless the dry pedagogue never existed save in the minds of the onlookers. Yet pupils of pre-Wells days have confirmed it. Perhaps close contact with the fine musical mind of Constant Lambert has helped her to set in order her own musical knowledge and to see beyond the actual construction.

De Valois' knowledge as a teacher does not stop at a very thorough understanding of classicism, or of music. She has both a knowledge of anatomy and an eye for line that enable her to diagnose and treat the slightest anatomical abnormality, a gift which has enabled her to develop much talent that would otherwise have been irretrievably lost.

I have mentioned de Valois' understanding of classicism, without which it would be impossible to be the leader of an Academy. De Valois, the rebel, not only had no such understanding but obviously very little sympathy for pure classicism. It is interesting to speculate when such a change came about. It seems reasonable to ascribe it to the influence of having a close contact with such a dancer as Alicia Markova, for whom *Giselle*, *Casse-Noisette*, and *The Swan Lake* were revived. Previously to that, de Valois' classical knowledge must have been confined to the rather sterile atmosphere of the classroom, a sound knowledge of the mechanics, since she was a prominent pupil of Cecchetti, but without an opportunity for artistic perception. During her period with Diaghileff, shortly after the sensational failure of *The Sleeping Princess*, the classics only existed in the one-act abbreviation, *Aurora's Wedding*, and classicism was at a low ebb. When Sergueeff revived these great works from his system of notation, the producer in de Valois must have played a large part in bringing them to life.

I have said that de Valois, like all pioneers and leaders of an artistic movement, has a one-track mind; it is also, in another sense, a large mind. The success of her own works is not her main preoccupation. She sees them almost impersonally, as one part of her main task. Never before in the history of repertory ballet have there been two resident choreographers working in close harmony. The case is still more difficult to conceive when one of them is a director of the company. De Valois has given to Frederick Ashton the most extraordinary support, whether she sees eye to eye with him or not. She has never denied to him the right of independent creation or even attempted to influence his productions. After a long experience of ballet, I marvel at the possibility of such a thing. That clear perception has meant that the Wells has been able to enlarge its scope in half the ordinary time.

De Valois is a thinker, a methodical worker in the great tradition of the *maîtres de ballet* of the past. She has outlined her ideas in a work of great value, *Invitation to the Dance*. It is vigorous, stimulating, and very revealing of her personality. The fighter and the rebel still exist alongside the successful leader of an Academy. It is both intolerant and infinitely understanding. It shows an exuberant temperament that can curb itself only to self-discipline, and de Valois' whole progress has been the steady acquiring of that discipline. She has made her rebel's nature richly creative. She overworks the entire time, but her work is planned and productive.

She is to-day the outstanding figure in the world of ballet; her accomplishment as a leader greater than anyone else's and certainly less disputed.

Her musical knowledge, her ability to express herself on paper, her choreography, pedagogy, and direction of a theatre bring one back to the heroic days, stressing once again the crying need for a higher education in dancing.

The Sadler's Wells School, which aims at the creation of a veritable conservatoire of ballet and the arts that compose it, will meet this need. To-day it looks after the dancer's complete education from the age of nine, and is similar in scope to the great Russian school that gave us a Pavlova and a Karsavina. *Lilian Baylis created a theatre that is more truly national than any State institution, since it was born out of the sixpences of the masses.*

II. MARIE RAMBERT

When the history of English Ballet, so recently born, comes to be written, the name of Marie Rambert will have an especially prominent position, for she it was who, pre-Camargo, pre-Wells, showed that the English girl had something to express as a dancer and was not merely fit for relegation to the back row of a Russian *corps de ballet*. It is not the Russians, by the way, who believed in the inferiority of the English girls, but the great British public itself. Sokolova, Markova, Dolin proved nothing; they were magnificent freaks; besides, they were very heavily disguised and not everybody knew the ghastly truth about their passports. Diaghileff himself believed in the English, marvelled at their aptitude, and said that one day they would have a ballet of their own.

Marie Rambert was the first to present a whole group of young *solistes* under their own, or at any rate British, stage names. They were interesting, these youngsters, and their youth itself was an extraordinary novelty. We had yet to meet de Basil and his babies. Providence was kind to English Ballet, allowing it four years between the last Diaghileff Season, Covent Garden, 1929, and the first de Basil Season, Alhambra, 1933, in which to be born and grow strong enough to continue life.

Marie Rambert came comparatively late to ballet, having specialized in the Dalcroze movement, and it was as an expert teacher of eurhythmics that she made her first contact with Russian Ballet. Whatever influence she may have had over the Russians, they completely won her over to ballet, and she became an ardent pupil of Cecchetti.

The fact that she started late and did not have much opportunity to practise her art has had an enormous bearing on her personality and has given her the burning desire to continue dancing vicariously. Marie Rambert is not a choreographer, and not a teacher in the ordinary sense of the word, but a frustrated dancer who makes others dance in her place. For this reason her influence has been genuinely creative.

After a season of public performances at which Karsavina consented to appear with her young prodigies, Marie Rambert started the Ballet Club, an old parish hall rebuilt and embellished by her husband, Ashley Dukes, into an elegant *bonbonnière* of a theatre. This was the first permanent home of ballet in England; a self-contained unit, a theatre with a company and a school of its own. There Frederick Ashton did his first important work, William Chappell discovered his gifts as a designer, Harold Turner danced *Le Spectre de la Rose* well enough for Karsavina to pick him as partner, and Pearl Argyle, Maude Lloyd, Prudence Hyman, Andrée Howard, Diana Gould, and others began to interest a limited but artistically influential public. The coming of the Russians did not kill it, though it removed some of the company, among them Vera Nelidova (née Betty Cuff) and Lisa Serova. The Ballet Club was one of the mainstays of the Camargo Society; in fact, together with Ninette de Valois, it *was* the Society, each one having a share in the indispensable Markova, who danced everywhere in those days, appearing for five minutes in a cinema for a substantial sum, dancing *Swan Lake* for love. The public has a strange sense of values at times.

The size of the Ballet Club stage has had a marked effect on Marie Rambert's work. It has denied her the culmination of her effort and its development to full maturity; also it has robbed her of much credit that is her due. Its advantages, and they exist, I will talk of later. The time must come when the dancer, and more especially the choreographer, grows cramped, physically and mentally. He requires the inspiration of an orchestra, a large stage, a big company, large audiences. If he does not feel this, there is something seriously wrong in his development. In the old days the goal was the Russian Ballet; to-day it is Sadler's Wells, and Marie Rambert has seen a number of her finest 'discoveries' express themselves most fully as truly mature personalities with Sadler's Wells: Argyle, Ashton, Turner, Chappell. Recently she has lost the products of a new generation, Belinda Wright and John Gilpin – to the Festival Ballet. She has had the uphill work of years, without the reward of seeing it finally coming to flower on her own stage.

Marie Rambert has immense flair for talent, and a nervous, vital enthusiasm. It seems to me that her *forte* has been in developing the very young whom she can guide artistically, and that her personality may prove too powerful for the artist who has passed the apprenticeship stage, resulting either in a conflict or in the submission of the artist, a bad thing, even when he is wrong. Marie Rambert is an acute analytical critic when her enthusiasm is held in check.

Where Marie Rambert has excelled is in seeing beyond the teaching of technique, in drawing out creative gifts. She is no choreographer, yet she taught Ashton, Anthony Tudor, Andrée Howard, Frank Staff, and Walter Gore to be choreographers; she made Chappell design. She has shown that a dancing-school must be something more than a physical-training ground: it must be a cultural centre. Her gifts of intelligence, culture, and wit have been of inestimable service to her pupils.

The advantages of the small stage are that experiment becomes economically possible. No one with a large theatre and an orchestra to pay can afford to take any risks. Russian

Ballet, to-day dependent on its own resources, has been relying for the most part on the choreographers developed by Diaghileff. Sadler's Wells is now too big a concern to risk a failure, but Marie Rambert can and must take risks. Temperamentally such a function suits her well, and she has the necessary flair to make it worth while. It is a significant fact, of which one might easily lose sight to-day, that from the first her experiments on that small stage were taken seriously by everyone and were never considered as pupil shows. She could have received no more genuine praise than that. Once the 'discoveries' are assets they will leave her; they may not be grateful to her – 'discoveries' so seldom are – but she will have had the satisfaction of the work itself.

Another field in which Marie Rambert has taken the lead is in the formation of a new branch of the art of ballet, the miniature or chamber ballet, and she has already sponsored some charming productions of that kind, the work of one of her original company, Andrée Howard, both designer and choreographer, who is able to make a virtue of the small stage and who, in *Death and the Maiden* and especially *Lady into Fox*, has created works of real skill and beauty.

Marie Rambert, more than anyone to-day, has set out with deliberation to find choreographic talent. She sees it latent in every pupil, she is boisterously optimistic, able to make others believe, including the would-be choreographer himself. And strangely enough, the talent often is there in sufficient quantity to reward her for her flair and courage.

III. FREDERICK ASHTON

Whenever a man accomplishes anything unusual, generally in the realm of crime, it is customary for the press to comment on the fact that he is a public-school boy. Frederick Ashton, after passing his youth in South America, was educated at a public school, a startling beginning to a successful career in ballet.

He started dancing by taking a lesson a week with Massine, and then joined Ida Rubinstein's company, coming under the influence of Nijinska. Those expensive ventures of Ida Rubinstein, eight months of rehearsal for a week of work, have proved of infinite importance in the history of contemporary ballet, giving us Lichine, Shabelevsky, Verchinina, Morosova, and others: a fact that should be placed to her credit.

Ashton must be considered a pupil of Marie Rambert, who gave him discipline, opportunity, guidance, and then a platform. He made his choreographic début in a revue at the Lyric, Hammersmith, with a small work, *The Tragedy of Fashion*. It was with the *Capriol Suite* and *Leda* that he showed marked ability. Pavlova greatly admired the former when it was shown by the Camargo Society, and came to a studio rehearsal of the latter. She was about to engage Ashton when she died so tragically.

It will be seen that Ashton enjoyed immediate recognition, and that his début was marked by an almost total lack of struggle. There was, however, a hard struggle to learn dancing at all, with an unhappy period in the city during which the precious time seemed to be slipping away. In this struggle Ashton revealed determination and character that were never missing even when he seemed to be enjoying a too great early success. He created each work with altogether extraordinary ease. The result was always highly effective theatrically, elegant, with an original angle, but somewhat derivative technically; first-class entertainment, but lacking in body. First for the Ballet Club, then for the Camargo Society, he produced a succession of works, many of which have survived, all of which met with success. His first large-scale production was *Pomona*. It launched the Camargo Society. It was definitely flippant, stylized Olympian, in a late Diaghileff vein, but it revealed the gift of being able to present his dancers to their very greatest advantage. This he followed up with *Façade*,[1] a still lighter work, but one that showed originality.

Ashton was from the first the very opposite of the other English choreographer, Ninette de Valois. She had a great deal to express and found difficulty in doing so; he had very little to say, but did so with extraordinary charm. She drew on her knowledge, he on his intuition. For a considerable period it looked as if he would go on eternally showing promise, spoilt by his own gifts. Everything he did was maddeningly charming and chic. Perhaps because he was criticizing himself at the time, he was bitterly resentful of criticism.

In America he met with great success from a small clique for his work in the Gertrude-Stein – Virgil-Thomson Opera, *Four Saints in Three Acts*. This American experience had a marked effect on his character. The enthusiastic praise of a clique of aesthetes, couched in the most extraordinary jargon, tickled his sense of humour. It was success of a type he no longer enjoyed. It gave him an entirely new set of values.

There is also no doubt that for a very long time he suffered from an inferiority complex, thinking of his own work in terms of the Russian Ballet and consequently rather despising popular success. This sense of inferiority completely vanished when he joined the flourishing Wells Ballet, and he not only enjoyed the advantages of a permanent company, but of the whole atmosphere of creation. It gave him something in which he could believe, and also threw him into close contact with Constant Lambert. Instead of having to rely upon scraps of music hastily thrown together, he could now collaborate with a man who understood the relationship between ballet and music more clearly than anyone else. Where before intuition had made his success, he could not call on knowledge to help him out. He could express far deeper emotions because

1. See page 168.

he felt them. He had become a conscious artist. Many of his works were still light, *Les Rendezvous*, for instance, but they formed a vivid contrast to what had gone before. For the first

time he was really grappling with his material, guiding it instead of making a surface effect. There was no need for strong external influences. He could listen to the music directly.

In *Nocturne* he showed genuine compassion; in *Apparitions* a vivid imagination disciplined by strong musical suggestions; in *Le Baiser de la Fée* a still further musical comprehension, his choreography bearing the same relationship to orthodox classicism as Stravinsky's music did to Tchaikovsky, upon which it was based. In *Horoscope* for the first time he handled his *corps de ballet* with maximum effect, showing himself a master of choreography.

This gain of conscious artistry has in no way lessened the feeling of spontaneity that he has always shown and that is one of his greatest qualities. *The Wedding Bouquet* appears to be a light-hearted frolic; only with close study does one see that the effects are obtained legitimately, out of movement, and that the dancing itself is splendidly sound.

In *Cinderella* (Prokofiev) and *Sylvia* (Delibes) Frederick Ashton has created our first full-length ballets, and so completed the journey that began with charming, elegant works conceived for individual artists. In these big ballets Ashton accepts a challenge. He must fill the stage, he must provide spectacle, he must deal with uninspired passages in a long score. Also he accepts the challenge in *Sylvia* of coping with period music without descending to pastiche; and never once does the movement he provides strike us as modern or as 'old world'.

No contemporary choreographer has shown a greater range. In *Tiresias*, his last partnership with Constant Lambert, there is an extraordinary feeling of Crete as the meeting-place of Egypt and Greece, conveyed without recourse to museum grouping, but revealing a completely assimilated lesson. In Ravel's *Daphnis and Chloë*, a difficult ballet because the music is too complete to need illustration, Ashton avoids the obvious eurhythmic Greece to throw in places a vivid new light on a score that had found Fokine uninspired.

Ashton is to-day a veteran choreographer, but there is still no successor in view.

IV. SERGE LIFAR

The key figures of contemporary ballet, subjects of this present chapter, are the heirs of Diaghileff. The question that we must always ask ourselves is what have they made with this inheritance?

We have seen that England adopted ballet and made a system out of Diaghileff's wonderful but precarious formula. Diaghileff's most faithful public was English, and many of his dancers were English when he was cut off from Russia and Poland, his main sources of supply. But with three small exceptions, *The Triumph of Neptune*, *The Gods go a-begging*, and *Romeo and Juliet*, he had never looked to England for any of the elements that make up ballet. Indeed, after the first, the Russian Benois–Bakst phase, all his inspiration had come from France, from what is loosely called *L'école de Paris*. It would not be unfair to have called the Diaghileff ballet from 1918 until the end 'Les Ballets Russes de Paris'. Yet there were no French dancers in the company, and the most ardent balletomane would have been hard put to give the name of a single French dancer of note. Yet the Opéra, cradle of all ballet, continued to house a large ballet company whose only *raison d'être* was to fill the stage in such a family spectacle as *Faust* or to provide decorative companions for cabinet ministers and business tycoons. Ballet was not a vocation for a respectable young woman, was not taken seriously as an art, except in the case of the visiting Russians. It was a stepping-stone, a way of getting on in life as Halévy's classic stories of Madame Cardinal and her daughters depict with such charm.

And this had been so since the decay of romanticism, and the disappearance of the magician Gautier and the ethereal beings of whom he wrote; I almost said, whom he had created.

England had to make a tradition, France to recreate one.

1. Anna Pavlova

2. *Pas de Quatre*

Alexandra Danilova

Mia Slavenska   Natalie Krasovska

Alicia Markova

3. Tamara Toumanova in *La Symphonie Fantastique*

4. Beryl Grey in *Swan Lake*

5. Margot Fonteyn in *Swan Lake*

6. Marjorie Tallchief

7. Moira Shearer as Aurora

8. Violetta Elvin in *Giselle*

9. Renée Jeanmaire

10. Alicia Markova

11. Alicia Markova in *Swan Lake*

12. Serge Lifar in *Icare*

13. Jean Babilée in *The Portrait of Don Quixote*

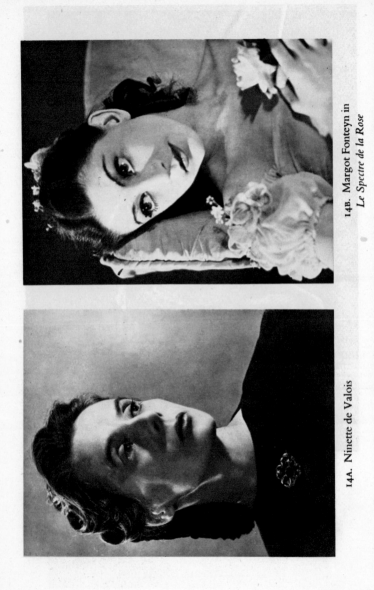

14B. Margot Fonteyn in *Le Spectre de la Rose*

14A. Ninette de Valois

15. Alexandra Danilova and Leonide Massine in *La Boutique Fantasque*

16. Alicia Markova and Igor Yuskevitch in *Giselle*

17. Rosella Hightower and André Eglevsky in *The Black Swan*

18. Nora Kaye as Lizzie Borden in *Fall River Legend*

19. Nora Kaye and Lucia Chase in *Pillar of Fire*

20A. Nina Vyroubova in *La Sylphide*

20B. Nina Vyroubova in *La Sylphide*

21. Yvette Chauviré in *La Mort du Cygne*

22. Renée Jeanmaire and Roland Petit in *Carmen*

23. Rosella Hightower and George Skibine in
Raymonda's Dream

24. Josette Clavier, a shade of Degas.
An unposed photograph taken at Alexandra Palace

The late André Levinson once wrote that Russia had repaid France for the loan of Petipa by sending Serge Lifar. That is true.

Serge Lifar was born in Kiev in 1905. He finished high school, studied the piano and violin at the conservatoire, and started to dance at the state school at the beginning of the revolution, where he learnt with Nijinska. He joined the Diaghileff Ballet in 1923, coming, an unwanted fifth, with a group of four boys for whom Diaghileff had sent. He made rapid progress under Maestro Cecchetti, and became *premier danseur* two years later. In 1929 he did his first piece of choreography, a new version of Stravinsky's *Le Renard*. In 1930 he joined the Paris Opéra as *premier danseur* and choreo-grapher, becoming professor two years later. With the excep-tion of a brief interval, 1944–6, he has ruled the Opéra ever since, creating for it some forty-five ballets, a large public, and a number of brilliant dancers; thus reviving the great French tradition.

Lifar's work is almost unknown outside France, and he is so controversial a figure that the foreign historian may easily overlook his outstanding position as one of the creators of contemporary ballet. We must not be led astray by some petty argument as to Lifar's political views by the fierce enmity that Lifar has created among some French critics, or by the fact that much of his choreography, often seen at a great disadvantage away from the Opéra, may not please us. The fact is that without him the very critics that assail him would not have a job at all. In England we know him through the dancers who have left the Opéra and his immediate influence. *It must never be forgotten that one of the functions of a true academy is to inspire rebels.*

Lifar gave the dancer in France a vocation, and laid the foundation for the work of Roland Petit, Janine Charrat, and such outstanding dancers as Yvette Chauviré, Renée

Jeanmaire, Jean Babilée. I could mention a score of others, including many at the Opéra itself, among whom is Josette Clavier.

It is another matter whether, for his own sake as well, Lifar's reign at the Opéra has been too absolute or too long, again a parallel with Petipa. His achievement is undeniable.

V. ROLAND PETIT

It is strange, and no doubt painful to both men, to have to say that Lifar re-created French ballet, but that we in England know French ballet not through Lifar but through Roland Petit, his one-time pupil at the Opéra. Moreover, it is Roland Petit who more than anyone else to-day has carried on the Diaghileff formula for ballet creation – the blending of the various elements that make up ballet and that, at frequent intervals, set off a balletic explosion.

Roland Petit, son of an Italian mother and a French father, was born in Paris in 1924. He joined the Opéra school, and was taken into the *corps de ballet* in 1939. He gave occasional concert performances during the war, with a group of artists who followed him. He left the Opéra in 1945 to form Les Ballets des Champs-Elysées. The art director of the company was Boris Kochno, so closely associated with Diaghileff's last years, and the very embodiment of the *École de Paris* and the 'snob' world, using that word in its very best sense. Petit's ballets made a tremendous impact on his audiences – often through the shock tactics that Diaghileff had loved so dearly. In *Le Jeune Homme et la Mort* he used a Bach Passacaglia as the background for a sordid, 'news-of-the-worldish' paragraph. His work has tremendous variety, from the moving, tender, beauty of *Les Forains* to that acid commentary on the classics, *Les Amours de Jupiter*. In 1948 Roland Petit severed his partnership with Boris Kochno and started his own Ballets de Paris. Many thought that he would be unable to carry the extra burden of acting as his own art director. They were wrong. He had thoroughly mastered the formula, and worked with as sure a touch as the experienced Kochno, creating such outstanding works as *Les Demoiselles de la Nuit*, *Carmen*, and *Le Loup*, as well as a large number of elegant and highly skilled trivialities such as *Œuf à la Coq* and *Deuil en Vingt-Quatre Heures*.

I am always surprised that so many of our critics stress the fact that Petit is abandoning serious ballet and being frivolous, acrobatic, and Casino-de-Parisish. The fact is that Roland Petit has created more major ballets in a shorter time than any of his contemporaries. By major ballets I am not talking of choreography alone, which, alas, in England is usually held to be synonymous with ballet. I mean, as I have already written, that a major ballet is the felicitous union of music, theme, décor, *and* choreography.

When Petit does do a minor work, he always gives us something that is highly professional in execution, and that calls upon first-class decorative artists, poets, and musicians. If they are out for a frolic and not working to create a masterpiece, it is all to the good. Petit is never boring, and his very elegance is all too rare to-day. Moreover, he is able to touch upon a *risqué* subject without the vulgarity and self-consciousness that all too often assails us and the Kinsey-Conscious Americans when we deal with sex. Roland Petit has much to teach us, even though he may seem to be the least didactic of choreographers and art directors. Petit's main risk is his speed and facility which may mean in the future that he does not get the very best out of himself, especially in the handling of a *corps de ballet*. He is already one of the chief architects of the contemporary scene.

VI. GEORGES BALANCHINE

Ballet in the twentieth century in the United States has never meant the same thing as in Europe. The Diaghileff Ballet had been seen through the waning star Nijinsky. The fame of Isadora Duncan and the experiments and importations of the eclectic Ruth St Dennis had turned the small dance-loving public in another direction. Ballet did not belong to the artistic world but to the spectacular music-hall show. Even though Fokine and other Russians had settled there and were teaching, they made little impact. The true creator of contemporary American Ballet and a major influence in the whole world of ballet to-day is Georges Balanchine.

Balanchine (full name Georgi Melitonovitch Balanchavadze) was born in St Petersburg in 1904. He entered the Imperial School in 1914; by the time he had graduated in 1921 it had changed its name to the Soviet State School of Ballet. Balanchine's father was a composer, and the young dancer studied composition and piano at the Leningrad Conservatoire. No other choreographer has so profound a knowledge of music.

He made his début as a choreographer in 1923 with a small group of dancers, among them Alexandra Danilova and Tamara Geva. In the following year the little company, under the name of the Russian State Dancers, took the opportunity of a foreign tour to escape into the free world. Curiously enough, Balanchine, like Fokine before him, was far too revolutionary for Russian audiences. In 1924 Balanchine and his dancers joined the Diaghileff Ballet. There he created such outstanding works as *La Chatte* (1927), *Apollon Musagète* (1928), *Le Fils Prodigue* (1929).

With the death of Diaghileff he became the first choreographer of the Monte Carlo Ballet, giving them *Concurrence* and *Cotillon* (1928), and discovering and launching Toumanova, Baronova, and the others. He next created a series of works for Edward James's *Les Ballets 1933*, among them *Mozartiana, Errante, Songes.*

At the end of 1933 Balanchine went to America, at the invitation of Lincoln Kirstein, to found the School of American Ballet, and ever since, in a number of ventures culminating in the New York City Ballet, these men have directed the course of ballet in America.

Balanchine has trained the American dancer, and has devised for her a neo-classicism that reveals her at her brilliant best. His series of ballets on well-known compositions – Concerto Barocco of Bach, Bizet Symphony in C, Tchaikovsky Piano Concerto No. 2, etc. – have inspired imitations all over the world, but rarely with success. Balanchine has gone back to the classicism of Petipa for his guide, feeling that everything that has happened since is dangerous as a foundation for the future. Balanchine's repertoire of movement is tremendous. Although he is known to our audiences mainly for the wrongly called 'abstract' ballets, which are in fact musical-interpretation ballets, he is equally a master in the narrative romantic ballet – *Night Shadows, Orpheus.*

As an art director as apart from choreographer, Balanchine has a tendency to neglect scenery and costume. This is partly due to financial reasons, partly to his feeling about the relationship of music and movement, but it does make much of his work untheatrical. I must confess that at the end of a long season of ballet and dancing of every type, I long for the logic and the purity of a Balanchine programme. His influence in America is supreme, but also outside America his influence on all choreography is evident and undoubted.

*

These, then, are the five architects of the contemporary scene. There are others whose influence can be felt – Anthony Tudor, the English choreographer who has become the father of what might be called the 'psychological ballet,' a hit-or-miss affair where in truth Tudor himself has made the only real hits with *Jardin au Lilas* and *Pillar of Fire*; and Agnes de Mille, who in *Rodeo* and *Fall River Legend* has brought American folk-lore to ballet. Her influence has been far more than a local one, thanks to the enormous success of the American musical, starting with *Oklahoma*.

VII. THE DANCERS

The dancers have always had an outstanding influence on ballet; e.g. Camargo and the aerial dance, Taglioni and romanticism, Pavlova and the new romanticism, the baby ballerinas and their *fouettés*. At times they are active collaborators with the choreographer, but even when they remain purely interpretative they play a large role in attracting the great public. At the present day, when the films have raided the ballet for 'stars', although the film-star dancers are not ballerinas and have contributed nothing to the main history of ballet, they have greatly influenced the economics of ballet, and are in a sense a real danger to the art.

A number of dancers have set their seal upon our period. I have already dealt with the phenomenal Pavlova and with the contribution made to the Diaghileff Ballet by Karsavina, the first of the moderns, and with Nijinsky. More recently I would say that Markova, Pearl Argyle, with Toumanova, Baronova, and Riabouchinska as representing the last of the *émigré ballet russe*, and Margot Fonteyn have had a real influence on the art of ballet. It is from that point of view alone that I write of them here. Experience has shown me that to discuss still-performing dancers from any other point of view in anything but a periodical is not practical, nor is it fair on the dancer.

Alicia Markova has enjoyed three distinct careers; as an Anglo-Russian child prodigy with Diaghileff (1925–9), as a pioneer English ballerina (1930–9, with the Camargo Society, the Ballet Club, the Sadler's Wells Ballet, the Markova Dolin company), and as a ballerina of travelling companies (1939 onwards), based mainly in the United States.

It is in her second period that Markova's great influence has been felt. English ballet was new; it lacked not only prestige but experienced dancers and choreographers. Markova brought with her, as well as her considerable prestige, the experience of having worked under Diaghileff's inspired direction with Balanchine, Nijinska, and Massine. She was young enough not to have become set in her ways. Her influence seems to me to have been equally strong in two directions. She proved an inspiration to the brilliant young Ashton, who created many roles for her (in *La Péri*, *Façade*, *Les Rendezvous*, *High Yellow*), and she made it possible for Ninette de Valois to put on the classics in their entirety, laying in this way the solid foundation of a national school. Without Markova, the whole history of our ballet would have been different.

The late Pearl Argyle, pupil of Marie Rambert, was not from a technical point of view a great classical dancer. She was, however, a sensitive and mature artist at the very moment that our English ballet needed someone who was not in any way connected with Russian Ballet. Frederick Ashton created some of his finest early romantic works for her (*The Lady of Shalott*, *Le Baiser de la Fée*, as well as his first ballet produced on a large stage, *The Birth of Venus* in Matheson Lang's *Jew Süss*), Andrée Howard and Anthony Tudor both created their first works for her, and, before any other dancer both at the Ballet Club and at the young Sadler's Wells, she convinced a sceptical public that the English dancer had something to express. Pearl Argyle had many notable contemporaries, among them Andrée Howard, Maude Lloyd, Diana Gould, Prudence Hyman, Harold Turner, and William

Chappell, but she stands out for the mature beauty of her work. In our history she fills the short gap between the reigns of Markova and Fonteyn.

I must now leave the English scene for a moment. If I have dwelt on our ballet, it is not for chauvinistic reasons, but because of the fact that our tradition is so very young that there are of necessity a number of artists who have played a part in laying its foundations and in dictating its style.

When the Diaghileff Ballet came to an end, it was in a sense the end of a whole period of art. It was still too soon to present to the public his ballets danced by his dancers with the only difference that both ballets and dancers were a trifle older. Diaghileff himself had said *à propos* of *Schéhérazade* that for a revival its colours would have to be made still more vivid, since memory invariably exaggerates. The public wanted a *ballet russe* that would thrill by its youth, novelty, and the extent of its technique. This was made possible by the young ballerinas who brought in the era of the *fouetté* and so gave *ballet russe* an Indian summer (see page 106 ff.).

These Russian children, born in Russia and settled in Paris from a tender age, were the pupils of Russian ballerinas comparatively unknown in Western Europe but the glories of the Imperial Ballet; Olga Pleobgrajenska taught Tamara Toumanova, Irina Baronova and others, Mathilde Kchessinska taught Tatiana Riabouchinska.

These Maryinsky ballerinas had concentrated on a hard classical technique, and had handed it down to their pupils, by-passing as it were the Fokine neo-romanticism. By great good fortune the receptive Balanchine was there to discover these pupils, launch them and make a use of them, in a way that no one else was to equal. This master took advantage of their very gaucherie and used them to launch the last period of *ballet russe* and a new period of ballet technique. Thanks to the work shown by them from 1933 onwards, the dancer of to-day has greatly extended her repertoire of movement. Their reign was too brief but their influence persists.

Now to return to the English scene. The choreographer, even when of the calibre of Ashton and de Valois, is limited by the material available. It is for that reason that the choreographer sees a school as an indispensable background to a company. Our young ballet had enjoyed magnificent good fortune in having, just when it needed them, Markova and Pearl Argyle with their widely differing gifts. It now needed someone who had grown with it and had been formed by it, an artist who would not only inspire its choreographers and reinterpret the classics but who would prove that given the material it could create. Such an artist revealed herself in 1935 when Margot Fonteyn stepped into the shoes of Alicia Markova, who had left Sadler's Wells to form a company of her own. A glance at the Sadler's Wells repertoire, creations as well as classics, will show the enormous influence of Fonteyn. The young dancers of to-morrow, the choreographers, and the critics are setting their standards from her just as my generation did from Pavlova, Karsavina, Nijinsky, Trefilova. And Fonteyn, who appeared with such fine artists created by Sadler's Wells as June Brae and Pamela May, is now surrounded by dancers of attainment, also products of the national school – among them Beryl Grey and Michael Somes.

There are many dancers of outstanding ability in the world to-day, so once more I must make it clear that those I have selected for mention are here for the sole reason of their influence on the direction of ballet itself.

CHAPTER SEVEN

Appreciation: Studies of some Ballets in the Contemporary Repertoires

(A practical application of Chapter Three)

IN this chapter I am going to comment on a series of ballets that are or have recently been in the regular repertoires of companies performing in England, studying them in the light of the background that forms the subject of the third chapter. I shall try to avoid the technique of the guide-book that marks special beauties with one or more asterisks. I have no wish to foist my own taste too obviously on the reader; my aim is to give him sufficient data to form a considered opinion of his own, to counterbalance, perhaps, the often uncritical emotions aroused by watching a very favourite performer who can do no wrong.

I will deal with the history, the conception, the music, choreography, and drama. The personalities who composed them are already known to us.

I. GISELLE

Romantic survival

Giselle, first presented in 1841, is the oldest ballet in the current repertoire, and has been given without interruption ever since its creation. Yet the history of its creation bears no hint that it was to be an enduring work.

Théophile Gautier, in reviewing Heine's *De l'Allemagne*, found himself fascinated by the legend of the *wilis* – maidens who have died before their wedding day and who come out of the graves at night in bridal dress to dance until dawn.

Should any man be caught in the wood when the *wilis* are dancing, he is doomed to dance on and on until he drops dead from exhaustion.

From Heine's description of the legend, Gautier saw an admirable theme for ballet, a romantic theme of beautiful women, white gauze, and German moonlight. Together with an experienced opera librettist, V. de Saint-Georges, he turned the theme into a story. The music by Adolphe Adam was written within a week, and the choreography devised as rapidly.

If we ask ourselves why this particular ballet has survived out of the countless works that enjoyed success, we shall be able not only to assess its particular value, but to learn something of ballet in general. The music does not account for the survival, though it is in every respect superior to the ballet music of its period. The most that one can say is that it has not prevented survival. It has to-day all the quaint charm of the romantic colour-print that one picks up for a few francs on the Paris quayside. The ballet as a whole also has its quaint moments, but it is very much more than a museum piece. It is a moving, living work. *Giselle* survives because it is the purest expression of its period, and because its story makes it the greatest of all tests for the ballerina. Every actress has the ambition at some time in her career to undertake the role of Marguerite Gautier in *La Dame aux Camélias*; every ballerina sees herself as *Giselle*. The parallel is exact in every particular. The old play is quaint, its mechanism is obvious, but it lives because it is magnificent theatre, and the chance it gives to the actress now delights Garbo or Yvonne Printemps as it did Sarah Bernhardt or Duse. The dancer in *Giselle* must have a very strong technical equipment, and in addition to that a great range of expression. She starts as a carefree village girl, fond of dancing and very much in love. Next, we see her betrayed and driven mad, until she dies a

Giselle.

suicide. Then, in the following act, she is a spirit who must impress upon us the fact that she is lightness itself and so make a vivid contrast with the red-cheeked villager of the first act. This acting raises innumerable difficulties. The scene of madness cannot be naturalistic or it would be altogether out of the picture. It must be lyrical and fit perfectly within the classical convention. The latitude allowed the actress is minute, every gesture is circumscribed. To succeed in *Giselle* means a triumph of personality, a unique example of true personality that is technically disciplined.

Another reason for its survival lies in the fact that it is more perfectly balanced than the other romantic ballets. The male role exists in fact, and is not merely inserted for purely technical reasons. Nijinsky made a name in this ballet, Lifar and Helpmann have both proved the dramatic possibilities of the part. *Giselle* is not merely an excuse for dancing, but lives on account of the drama that it expresses. Of all the romantic ballets, one can rely only upon contemporary accounts; it stands alone in fulfilling the conditions laid down by Noverre.

Within living memory Pavlova was supreme in the role. To have seen her in nothing else is to have seen every facet of her art. She made one innovation to increase the plausibility of the scene, dancing the second act in draperies suggestive of grave clothes, instead of in the conventional ballet skirt. Unfortunately, her innovation was abandoned. It is both logical and in a tradition that is older and more acceptable than that of the middle nineteenth century. After Pavlova only certain aspects of the complex role have been revealed. Olga Spessivtseva (Spessiva) has danced it with magnificent purity of line; Markova, for whom it was revived in England, gave a deeply moving rendering, especially of the second act; Margot Fonteyn has stressed the tenderness of the character and more nearly resembles Pavlova than any other dancer I have seen in making one forget the mechanics of the ballerina. Yvette Chauviré has brought back the feeling of the period as no other dancer has done. Her *Giselle* is a living romantic lithograph.

To dance *Giselle* with any degree of success is to be a considerable dancer and an artist as well. The conception of the role rises above the quaint appealing music and the conventionally effective setting. The ballet lives because its central figure is a genuine character whose suffering can move one to compassion. The poetic inspiration of Heine and Gautier has shone through what has become a dead formula.

II. THE SWAN LAKE: AURORA'S WEDDING

Classical survivals

The Swan Lake was first produced in 1877. It was of considerable importance and well ahead of its time in conception, since it meant that once again the serious composer was to be concerned in the making of ballet. Admirable though it is choreographically, its survival is certainly due to the music of Tchaikovsky. The only works of the period to survive are those by Tchaikovsky: *The Swan Lake*, *Casse-Noisette*, and *The Sleeping Princess*. At the time, his music was considered too symphonic in form to be suitable for the theatre. That alone reveals to us the true state of ballet and balletomanes.

The original production was a failure, and it was only after the composer's death that the work succeeded, when it was revived in 1894, with fresh choreography by Petipa, thanks to the enlightened rule of I. A. Vsevolojsky, director of the Imperial Theatres.

The Swan Lake presents an enormous contrast to *Giselle*. It is not so essentially romantic, though its music is truly romantic in contrast to the tuneful tinkle of *Giselle*. It has a story of the conventional romantic type with a heroine of dual personality who has been bewitched by an evil spirit.

The story, however, is of no account. It is told, like *Giselle*, by means of conventional miming, but whereas in *Giselle* the actress-dancer can convey a depth of meaning outside the

mime, in *The Swan Lake* the mime remains as a rather tedious interruption of the dancing; so much so that in many versions it has been heavily curtailed, and with no loss. The essence of *The Swan Lake* is its dancing, and the role was created for the greatest virtuoso of her day, Pierrina Legnani. It was her *fouettés* that caused a sensation, and not her acting.

Today, *The Swan Lake* in its entirety survives in Russia, the home of old-fashioned ballet, and at Covent Garden. The version that is best known is that used by Diaghileff, a concentrated affair in one act. This, while it makes the ballet more acceptable to modern ideas, slightly distorts it, and the tendency has been more and more to attack it in the spirit of *Les Sylphides*, giving it a softness alien to Petipa and his period. This one-act abbreviation dispenses entirely with one aspect of the heroine's dual nature, the hard facet in which she dazzles the Prince by her virtuosity. It dispenses also with the conventional act of *divertissements*, where a ball or celebration is used as an excuse to introduce various dances for their own sake, intruding on the narrative. The essence of the classical ballet is a very positive narrative that is disregarded in favour of showing as many aspects of dancing as possible. Ballet classicism departs a long way from the great masters who founded the art, and is to that extent misnamed.

In *Aurora's Wedding*, the other Petipa-Tchaikovsky survival, all that remains is the series of disconnected dances. In this respect it reveals the classical principle much more clearly than *The Swan Lake*. Diaghileff took the celebration scene from the full-length *The Sleeping Princess*,[1] and added to it many dances from *Casse-Noisette*. That alone shows us the looseness of classical construction: dance for the sake of dancing, any excuse is justified so long as the dance itself is harmonious. Princess Aurora herself has no existence as a character. At her own wedding she is merely the *ballerina assoluta*. The second most important personages in the ballet, the Blue Bird and the Princess, appear only in the last act. Their dance

1. The complete *Sleeping Beauty* has been one of the Sadler's Wells triumphs since the first night of the revival at Covent Garden on February 20th, 1946.

is one of the gems of ballet, but if it were cut out entirely it would not in any way alter the story of *The Sleeping Princess*. Also, even considered as a dramatic entity, the dance of the Blue Bird has no significance. Fokine's *Dying Swan* is a drama, Petipa's Blue Bird and Princess are brilliant dancers. Like a large canvas by Ingres, master of the French classical school of painting, this dance charms us by its line, delights us through its composition, but leaves us emotionally cold.

It must not be imagined on this account that these dances call for nothing but an accomplished technique. They also make considerable demands on artistry and personality. Nothing can more easily be rendered vulgar than the Blue Bird or Aurora's *pas de deux*, if the dancer concentrates on the steps at the expense of the dance as a whole. Apart from technical ability, the quality to be looked for in these classical dances is an interpretation that removes them from acrobatics,[1] that gives them dignity and purity. If the ballet has no entity of plot or structure, each dance apart has a structural entity, and the great classical dancer is the one who realizes that conception.

III. LES SYLPHIDES: LE SPECTRE DE LA ROSE

The new romanticism

Les Sylphides, the best-known and the most constantly danced of all ballets, is an expression of the reaction in Fokine against the artificialities of classicism. It does not react against classical technique but against the paraphernalia that surround it. It is a return to romanticism, to the true spirit of romanticism and not to its period expression. The period expression of romanticism dates; its works, with the exception of *Giselle*, are dead; but the romantic spirit itself survives at every period and in every art.

1. See page 43.

Les Sylphides

Les Sylphides as first conceived by Fokine had a standard romantic setting, the coming to life of images in the mind of the fevered composer. Later, in 1908, it became the suite of dances that we know to-day, and Diaghileff altered its original title of *Chopiniana* to that of *Les Sylphides* for its presentation during his first Western European season, Paris, 1909.

The title, suggested by Taglioni's famous ballet *La Sylphide*, is particularly apt, for in *Les Sylphides* is preserved all that was best in *le ballet blanc*. Though the work is composed of various disconnected dances (Chopin *Nocturne*, opus 32, No. 2; *Valse*, opus 70, No. 1; *Mazurka*, opus 33, No. 3; *Mazurka*, opus 67, No. 3; *Prelude*, opus 28, No. 7, also used as the overture; *Valse*, opus 64, No. 2; and *Valse*, opus 18, No. 1), it is not a *divertissement*. It has an absolute unity of atmosphere. The use of the *corps de ballet*, making them into expressive artists instead of a mechanical background, not only connects the whole, but distinguishes the new romantic ballet from the classical and romantic works of the past.

The Swan Lake calls in the first place for the interpretation of a dance; *Les Sylphides* demands more; it demands the interpretation of music. Though it has no direct dramatic narrative, through this work the ghost of Noverre is at last appeased. Logic enters once more into ballet; music, atmosphere, movement, and costume are gloriously reunited.

Le Spectre de la Rose

In this small work the shade of Théophile Gautier revisits the scene of his triumphs, and with it he enjoys a posthumous success. So perfectly conceived is it, so delicate, making such demands on its interpreters, that to-day, though constantly given, it scarcely exists. It demands a dancer of exceptional virtuosity who will subordinate himself to the role. The leap out of the window that the audience has concentrated upon and will insensitively applaud has killed the ballet. Fokine invoked romanticism, the audience has insisted upon classicism, and has been satisfied.

This ballet, to Weber's *Invitation à la Valse*, directly inspired by a poem of Gautier's, tells the story of a young girl returning from her first ball. She drowses, and the spirit of the red rose that she has been given comes to life and dances with her and then disappears. It is an experience that happens but once in a lifetime. She awakes disillusioned. The maiden has become a woman. This ballet, properly understood, is the most perfect theatrical expression of adolescence. Its misunderstanding is due to the fact that while dramatically the leading role is the woman's, from the dancing point of view the lead is the man's. To-day, neither dancers nor audience realize that fact. The man, the spectre of the rose, is dramatically on the second plane, a projection of the woman's dream. Only if this is made clear by the dancers does the ballet survive. The force of the woman's acting must eclipse the brilliance of the man's dancing, and the role is an exceptionally quiet one that calls for no obvious acting but that must carry with it both conviction and sincerity. However brilliantly Nijinsky danced, the triumph was Karsavina's, and she succeeded in recapturing it on every occasion, even when she danced with admittedly inferior partners. In difficulty the role is equalled only by that of *Giselle*. It calls for less sustained effort and for less technique, but for a far more subtle understanding of dramatic values. Since Karsavina, no dancer has deliberately succeeded; many ballerinas have made of it a dismal failure. Only certain immature dancers have instinctively captured something of the mood. If the audience would show more understanding and not applaud the leap in the middle of the girl's sad awakening, the ballet would have a greater chance of survival.

IV. CARNAVAL

Porcelain mischief; another aspect of the new romanticism

Fokine's *Carnaval* to Schumann's music of the same name was composed hastily in 1910 for a charity entertainment, and was taken into the Diaghileff repertoire the following year.

It is slight, subtle, witty, tender, and pathetic; a quickly changing pattern of moods. Every dancer must be the interpreter of a carefully conceived role, in which period style plays its part. Delicate as porcelain, to-day it has 'come to pieces in me 'and', and though it has been stuck together again, the rivets are painfully obvious. Ballets of this type can be preserved only when there is leisure to educate the dancers. For that reason the version given at Sadler's Wells, though far from satisfactory, since it has not had the advantages of direct contact with Fokine, is the most consistent to be seen to-day. The interpretation of *Carnaval* calls for infinite attention to detail. The fault of most productions is that the roles tend to become blurred and assume one another's characteristics. It would be difficult to imagine anything farther from dancing for the sake of dancing. Every little movement is an expression of character: Pierrot, lumbering and dejected, sentimental and credulous; Columbine and Harlequin playing the same game at the expense of the other characters, carefree and heartless, exploiting their brilliance and charm; Chiarina, also a flirt, more sentimental, deceiving herself at times; Pantalon, vain and pompous, the clubman ' 'pon my word'; Papillon, flitting brilliantly through to mock at Pierrot. To-day, the Philistines who intrude upon the scene and make themselves the butt of all the characters, have very little meaning. We know 'highbrows' and 'lowbrows', but both are drab, both sneer at the romantic, and would be the butt of Fokine's enchanted and enchanting characters.

Biedermeyer Germany is dead for ever – William killed it before Hitler – and *Carnaval* is as much the essence of Biedermeyer as *Giselle* is the essence of the more robust romanticism of its period. Bakst's delicate setting is an indispensable part of the ballet. Two attempts to use a new setting totally destroyed the work. The very fact that they should have been attempted showed a lack of understanding. *Carnaval* can only be understood by dancers and audience if it is seen as the definite expression of a period. Perhaps it will never really come to life again.

V. SCHÉHÉRAZADE: THAMAR

Exotics

Romanticism has always been interested in the exotic, and such ballets as *Revolt in the Harem* enjoyed a tremendous popularity. The new romanticism also turned to the exotic, and the flaming macaw-wing colours of Léon Bakst revolutionized decorative art.

There is nothing more dangerous dramatically than the exotic, which all too easily becomes ludicrous, like the Oriental department of a large emporium, and loses the essential plausibility. I have already discussed the genesis of *Schéhérazade*. To many it will seem slightly old-fashioned, in the sense that it does not create the overwhelming impression it once did; but no one can find it comical, as they did *Cleopatra* when it was revived. The orgy is convincing. Cecil de Mille has yet to equal it, in spite of the lavish nature of his entertainments.

Schéhérazade is brilliantly constructed round Rimsky-Korsakov's symphonic poem. Its blood-curdling narrative is well told, its characters wonderfully indicated. We know the imperious, sensual, vicious Zobeide, the kindly, weak, credulous Shah, his sceptical brother, as well as if they had spoken three acts of dialogue. They are 'round' characters. How expressive the movement of the Shah's brother in kicking the body of the dead slave, as if to say, 'You are about to forgive her and she gave herself to this'. How telling the final scene between Zobeide and the Shah, an admirable example of what can be narrated through mime when it is handled by a master. The eunuch alone is 'flat', a conventional comedy figure. He only accentuates the reality of the others. Finally, there is the study of the slave himself, the completely physical man, whom only ballet could exploit to the full. But characterization alone would make this into a pantomime. It has far more than narrative value. There is a richness of design that is interesting and logical in itself, movement that is exciting in itself apart from what it tells us. The slave's leap on to the cushion is an exciting athletic feat, as well as a demonstration of character. And Bakst's colours are a part of the music and the story. It is impossible to remove any element from this ballet without causing the collapse of the whole. The type of romanticism of *Schéhérazade* is far removed from us to-day, but *Schéhérazade* remains completely convincing, a vivid lesson in ballet composition.

Cleopatra has failed to survive. Its story is worth that of *Schéhérazade*, some of its dances are exceedingly powerful, and Bakst's décor and costumes are good. It has failed because the music is a weak collection of hackneyed tunes, carrying no conviction. What should be pathetic has become comical, and we await in vain the entrance of Nervo and Knox to complete the fun.

Thamar, exotic sequel to *Schéhérazade*, still survives. Balakirev's music is superior to Rimsky-Korsakov's, but not as ballet music. It lacks the directness. It tells the story in its own way, more completely. It is contemplative music rather than action music. *Thamar* is the study of one woman, and it lives only if that woman is a consummate actress. Its dances are, in a sense, a very conventional stage version of Caucasian folk-dances. There are none of the rich creations of *Schéhéra-zade*. *Thamar* is never ridiculous, but it is only just alive.

VI. THE POLOVTSIAN DANCES FROM
PRINCE IGOR

The restoration of the male dancer

The Polovtsian Dances from Borodin's opera, *Prince Igor*, more than anything secured the triumph of Diaghileff's Russian Ballet in Western Europe. An analysis of the first Paris press, 1909, clearly shows that the focal point was this essentially virile ballet.

When the Russian Ballet first came to Paris, its triumph was by no means assured. Ballet still survived at the Opéra, and Paris had seen many brilliant ballerinas. The male dancer no longer existed as an artist. The romantic credo and the out-standing success of Taglioni had reduced him to a secondary role. Romanticism in Russia had never gone to such extremes. Through the serfs, ballet had kept touch with reality. Ballet was not the plaything of poets. It had a solid contact with the people. Of the two brothers Petipa, Lucien remained in France and earned praise because he never obtruded himself; Marius went to Russia and became the Tsar of ballet.

Ballet, as we have shown, has as one of its ingredients *the orchestration of dancing*. Without the male dancer that orches-tration is impossible. Male movement is the complement of female movement. When an all-male ballet performed in London it defeated its own object: it did not reveal male movement. Without any contrast the result was meaningless and monotonous. The weaker males were almost forced into the position of female impersonators. The result is equally bad in an all-women ballet. Not only is the physical balance upset, but the dramatic as well, even when there is no concrete narrative. The *pas de deux* is more than a physical contrast: it is a love duet. There is this feeling of courtship in every *adagio*, even if it is as coldly classical as in the dance of the Blue Bird or as sublimated as in *Les Sylphides*.

For this very reason it may be taken as axiomatic that *the effeminate male dancer is a bad dancer*. There are altogether too many effeminate dancers in ballet. Effeminacy has become a bad tradition during the last twenty years, and is to-day causing untold damage, turning the virile athletic boy away from an art in which he could excel. Perhaps because dancing and the spirit of the old school tie, 'play the game, you cads', seem so far removed, English male dancers are particularly effeminate, a very serious danger. Ballet originated with men, and is in no way incompatible with virility. Grace must not be confused with effeminacy: Carpentier was one of the most graceful creatures I have ever seen.

Prince Igor suddenly convinced Western Europe of the existence of the male dancer. His position in character ballet was immediately clear, but a misunderstanding still persists as to his role in classical or romantic ballet. A romantic costume does not make a man effeminate. The most swashbuckling males wore what we would now term romantic costumes. Whatever his costume, the role of the male in ballet is that of a lover, and his physical attributes must be those of the star athlete. An understanding of this is essential. Without it ballet is in grave danger.

VII. PETROUCHKA

The perfect dance drama

I have already written at some length of the origin of *Petrouchka*. It is indeed difficult not to quote it at all times as the perfect expression of the dance drama, rich in theme and colour, in character and pattern. It is the most truly Russian of

Marionettes do not look alive to anyone at all times. The perfect expression of the doll always varied with its movement, expression, distance, and pattern. It is the same with those of —

all Russian ballets, its music and dancing inspired by the soil.

Its construction is interesting; a background of walkers-on who move and act but do not dance and who exist as individuals; next, the nurses, the coachmen, and the other characters who are also a part of the crowd, but who perform set national dances; and in the foreground the actors in the drama: Petrouchka, the Moor, the Ballerina, and the Charlatan. The audience is introduced to the characters first through the eyes of the spectators, then it is privileged to witness the drama as its develops behind the curtains of the booth, then once again it forms a part of the crowd to see the resulting murder, straying behind to watch the final triumph of Petrouchka. In this way the story is told from two angles and in complete detail. The whole thing is so simple that there is no need to refer to the programme for guidance, yet much more is expressed in the action than could ever be expressed in words. The characters are vividly contrasted: the Dancer, a heartless coquette; the Moor, a savage, strong and very physical, terrified of the unknown; Petrouchka, striving to express himself, in love with beauty, sawdust finding a soul. The jostling, merry crowd of the first scene only accentuates the claustrophobia of poor Petrouchka in the second scene: one of the most pathetic to be seen on the stage. Although there are a number of seemingly independent dances, not one is there merely as an embellishment. They are all necessary to situate and to underline the tragedy. *Petrouchka* is told with extraordinary economy. *Le Coq d'Or*, equally Russian in theme, is verbose in parts, much of it is frankly spectacle. *The Firebird* is a fairy-tale far more poetically expressed, in every way a superior work, but *Petrouchka* stands alone. It is the *Hamlet* of ballet.

*

These Fokine ballets are the standard works of the repertoire. It is necessary to know them thoroughly before understanding ballet. A proportion of them must have been studied by every serious dancer, and those who have not interpreted their leading roles cannot be called ballerinas. The fact that they were composed before the first World War does not mean that ballet has produced nothing since. What it does mean is that the dancer of to-day and the public of to-day have been brought up on them, that their continued and uninterrupted popularity testifies to their merit, and that they are performed by more than one company. They satisfy certain essential conditions so that, no matter how ballet develops, they will not lose their interest. Survival is an infallible proof of merit. Nothing could appear more old-fashioned to-day than certain of the ballets of the last Diaghileff period. They were amusing novelties, but bad works of art. The really fine work, unless lost by accident, expresses a constant truth.

I am going to comment on some of the more recent ballets that have points of special interest and that are to be seen almost every year.

The next group of ballets – they can also be called standard works – are selected from the great number created by Massine.

VIII. THE THREE-CORNERED HAT

And the 'translation' of raw material

Spain, one of the few countries open to the Russian Ballet during the 1914 War, had a marked influence on Massine, since most of his formative period had been passed there. He had from the first produced various small works in the Spanish manner. Diaghileff had long been an admirer of Spanish dancing, and was in close touch with Picasso and Manuel de Falla. The result of all this was inevitably a Spanish ballet. Massine learnt the technique of the dance from a Seville gipsy, Felix by name. It has been said that this Felix, who subsequently went insane, was ill-used, and actually composed the ballet. To anyone who has followed the argument of this book such a supposition is clearly absurd. Felix supplied the basic material, but he could be no partner to a Picasso or a de Falla. *The Three-Cornered Hat* is a highly sophisticated work, a translation of Spanish folk-dancing into terms of the theatre. It could have been created only by an experienced choreographer. Massine used Felix's material, just as in other ballets he used the material of ballet classicism or of the museum.

This question of 'translation' is all-important. Picasso did not copy traditional Spanish costume, he 'translated' it for the stage; de Falla 'translated' folk-music. The groundwork of *Petrouchka* is likewise a 'translation' of Russian folk art. It could not have been created by a dancing coachman. Diaghileff, who more than anyone possessed both the instinct and the understanding of the theatre, always maintained that nothing is less convincing than the real thing brought on to the stage. A case in point was the ballet *Children's Tales*. A real horse brought on to the stage where everything else was stylized looked fantastic and out of place. It was necessary to 'translate' the horse and to substitute a wooden one, which immediately fitted into the scheme. I have myself never seen anything more ridiculous than an elephant introduced on to the stage in an American picture-house version of *Schéhérazade*. It made everything else look unreal. There are a number of Spanish dancers of exceptional virtuosity and artistry to whom the farucca in *The Three-Cornered Hat* would be child's-play, but they could never make the impression of the Russian ballet dancer Massine. They might not even appear so Spanish. Their artistry is spontaneous and intuitive, his entirely conscious.

The failure of *Gaieté Parisienne* is due to a lack of this very 'translation' in which Massine usually excels.

IX. LA BOUTIQUE FANTASQUE

And the creation of character

La Boutique Fantasque, first presented in 1919, was planned in Italy during the war. Diaghileff decided to make a ballet out of certain pieces that Rossini had composed in his old age for the amusement of his guests. André Derain was chosen for the décor and costumes, and immediately proved himself a theatrical designer of the front rank.

The subject of toys coming to life at night is an old and obvious one for ballet. Pavlova had long made *The Fairy Doll* popular; but the music was too poor and the choreography too mechanical for it to have any existence as a work of art without her.

Massine brought an entirely fresh point of view to his choreography. He gave his toys character, avoiding the pitfalls of purely mechanical movement. From the very moment that we see them first of all as toys in the shop they have in them the possibility of independent life. The thing is so plausible that when it happens we are both charmed and convinced. The old shopkeeper is at first glance a ballet-type comic, but when he develops in his by-play with the young assistant, a typical Italian street urchin, we soon realize that he is a personality. The same with the Englishman and the Russian and their families. Observe how the Russian father counts and pays out the money. Even the maiden aunt is drawn in full. This ballet lives because it tells a familiar story in an unfamiliar way. We can make a not too far-fetched comparison with a novel by Dickens, a familiar theme enriched by the creation of a whole gallery of characters in the middle of which there is a delightfully sentimental episode.

The richness of the choreography is astonishing. Massine has 'translated' movement from Italy, Russia, France, from the streets, from toys and paintings. There is never a moment of monotony, and music and décor are of a piece. The famous can-can requires a pure classical dancer to interpret it and once again reveals the infinite variety of ends to which the classical system is a means.

X. LE BEAU DANUBE[1]

Massine's tour de force

This ballet was devised by Massine immediately after his choreography for *Le Sacre du Printemps*, a complex work of incredible difficulty. It came to him easily, almost as a necessity, and at a time when jazz and not the Viennese waltz was the order of the day.

It seems obvious to construct a ballet round the melodies of Johann Strauss. It is so obvious that many have tried it, and failed. This music is almost a too complete expression of the dance itself. In *La Boutique Fantasque* the theme was obvious; here the music is, and once again Massine has accomplished a *tour de force* by creating a whole gallery of living people, and so telling a sentimental anecdote with remarkable style.

These characters are human and lovable. There is an interesting contrast between the two women who love the hussar: the timid young girl and the bold street dancer. The street dancer is vulgar, but once again the role calls for a pure classical dancer. The vulgarity must be balletic, never actual. One of the most remarkably conceived roles is Massine's own hussar. It is wrong to conceive of a ballet in terms of an individual dancer. I must be allowed to make of this case an exception. There is a moment in the story when the hussar stands in the centre of the stage motionless, reflecting while the other characters dance round and mock at him. That lack

1. This refers to the original version before crude decoration ruined the balance of the work. – A. L. H.

of motion must be positive; with nearly every dancer lack of motion is negative. Massine and Helpmann almost alone possess this particular quality. When Massine stands there on the stage he becomes the focal point; when any other dancer ceases to move he vanishes from our attention. Massine reveals this quality in two other roles. In *The Three-Cornered Hat* when the Miller's Wife is dancing and he is a spectator, he shows such positive concentration that he enhances her dance by making the actual audience concentrate. In *La Symphonie Fantastique*, when he is watching the pastoral movement one can feel that it is a part of his own life. These are the great moments of ballet, so subtle that they cannot be rewarded by applause; but they distinguish the true artist from the competent dancer.

Le Beau Danube is a fine enough ballet to make its effect without Massine, but without him it loses in meaning and intensity.

XI. MAM'ZELLE ANGOT

A period frolic

Leonide Massine's *Mam'zelle Angot*, based on Lecocq's enchanting operette, shows an extraordinary combination of wit and humour, and a masterly knowledge for period style. As in all Massine's ballets, it is highly complex in movement, so that it requires many visits in order to appreciate all its subtle detail, and to notice how Massine, as always, has drawn on the painting of the period. Yet in spite of its complexity its effect is as immediate as half a pint of champagne, and very similar in character. This is not just a costume piece, but something that is impregnated throughout with the style of directoire France. One of the *pas de deux*, however, is too acrobatic to match the lightheartedness of the music, and seems out of the picture. It was put in, however, with delibera-

tion, as revealing the grotesque character of the caricaturist;
over-subtlety that failed. The finale with its riot of complex
movement is one of the choreographer's very happiest efforts.

Closely collaborating with him is his old partner, André
Derain, the most distinguished stage designer of to-day; and
Derain excelled himself. Like Massine, his work repays close
study, but the general effect is immediate, and he has performed that very difficult feat of translating a period of definite style into terms of the ballet stage. His work should be
studied by all young designers, most of whom seem to believe in embellishments and decoration, rather than in a complete picture that is a part of the whole.

Gordon Jacob's skilled orchestration plays a large part in
the success of this enchanting work.

XII. LA SYMPHONIE FANTASTIQUE

Five ballets in one

La Symphonie Fantastique was presented at Covent Garden
in 1936 after many years' planning.

Although a choreographic version of Berlioz' *Symphony*, it
did not arouse the customary controversy, since the composer himself laid down a programme and foresaw the possibility of its production in theatrical form.

Nothing shows Massine's versatility and skill better than
this ballet in five parts, each part of which is a distinct ballet.

The first part is the true symphonic ballet of the *Choreartium* type, though there is no abstraction. In its grouping
and pattern it reaches great heights, and it has a unity lacking
in *Choreartium*, since all the action centres round the person of
the Musician and seems to flow from him. Its faults are those
inherent in symphonic ballet: certain beginnings and endings
of movements and lifts for which the music has no equivalent
and which suddenly jar and shock. The setting, by Bérard,

immediately strikes the right romantic note, but the costumes again present a problem; those same draperies and tights that we have come to think of as 'symphonic costume', which require bare feet, arms, and legs to be really in keeping.

The second movement, in the ballroom with its swirling couples waltzing, is more conventionally balletic, because the music is more definitely dance music. The scene is a beautiful and satisfying thing in itself, but it rather loses sight of the drama. The dance beguiles us so much that the quest of the Musician for his Beloved becomes a secondary matter. Ashton, who has treated the identical subject in *Apparitions*, has made his ballroom scene more moving by treating his whirling couples as a background to the drama.

The white costumes against the red colonnaded room are not merely striking in themselves, but belong to the ballet, a rarity in these works where the music dictates the whole manner.

The third movement presented the greatest problem of all, through both its length and its type. The first movement spoke of conflicting emotions, the second was a waltz; this third tells a story, but not in direct narrative. The Musician is feeling, groping his way. He has halted by a pastoral scene, beguiled by its serenity. He sees his ideal, but she is only an image. It is the last period of calm before the violence to come, and a hint of that violence is conveyed by the sudden gusts of wind. Listening to the music, the problem of presenting parallel action to so ruminative a mood seems insoluble. Yet Massine has succeeded in creating some of the noblest choreography of this generation: the only pastoral ballet that is convincing. He has fully grasped the mood and attempts no direct narrative. The Musician is there, a passive figure, but one who dominates the action dramatically, though not physically. It is obvious that the action we are watching is being seen through his eyes and is closely related to his sorrows. When he leaves the stage nothing but the wind remains. In this scene Massine tells the whole story. It is complete in itself, a deeply moving study of artistic frustration.

The next scene, where the Musician who has murdered his Beloved is tried and executed, the famous death march, is the most obviously dramatic; the first to tell a direct narrative. Bérard, the painter, has collaborated admirably with Massine in presenting a period picture, the biting satire of Daumier. The judges are executioners, the executioners sadists. The Musician indicates that the suffering is moral as well as physical. This act treats social satire in very much the same manner as Kurt Jooss has done in *The Green Table*. It is a new departure in Russian Ballet.

The final act, a witches' sabbath, the struggle between Church and hell for the Musician's soul, is in some respects the weakest dramatically, though for complexity of detail and pattern it is worthy of a Breughel or Hieronymus Bosch. This scene, so much a set-piece of the Romantic period, has been treated many times recently. Ashton was the first to do so in *Apparitions*; then Fokine in *Don Juan*; and Nijinska in *The Legend of Cracow*. Fokine's version was simpler and more immediately effective, because the eye could take in the whole at a first glance; but Massine has conveyed better than anyone the danger to the soul as apart from the danger to the body. The moment where the Beloved has turned into a witch is one of the most gruesome in all ballet. With repeated viewings this scene grows greatly in intensity, and the manner in which the choreographer has indicated the medievalism of the Second Empire is an extraordinary *tour de force*.

La Symphonie Fantastique as a whole is a monumental work.

There is yet another group of works with which I propose to deal. They are in the repertoires of our national companies at Covent Garden and Sadler's Wells and have a considerable importance, not only because they are good in themselves, but because they are landmarks in the development of English Ballet. They may be considered standard works in the sense that I have been using the word. Other important works in this repertoire have already been dealt with in the sketches of their creators.

XIII. JOB: THE RAKE'S PROGRESS: BAR AUX FOLIES BERGÈRE

Inspiration from painting

Job, to music by Vaughan Williams, was created for the Camargo Society by Ninette de Valois. It is a smart thing to call this an admirable work and then to say, 'but of course it is not a ballet'. On the programme itself it is styled a masque, which is also inaccurate. Such nomenclature has very little importance, but it must be corrected or it leads us on a false trail. If *Job* is not a ballet, then there are only a score of ballets in existence to-day. There is an idea that ballet must consist of a series of set dances, and if those dances do not follow in quick succession and are not underlined so that the veriest tyro cannot miss them, it becomes the thing to say, 'There is not enough dancing in this ballet'.

Job is all dancing; movement guided by music is dancing and nothing else. It is essential to understand once and for all that in ballet, just as in opera, there is *aria* and *recitative*. *Job* has its grand aria, Satan's dance; it has magnificent choral passages, and it uses recitative.

It tells the story of *Job* in terms of Blake, an extremely risky thing that has here succeeded beyond a doubt. The work of a painter is static, the choreographer must make it move, but always in the spirit of the painter. He must, in fact, paint thousands of pictures in his manner. Already the nature of the art binds de Valois to the music; when she seeks pictorial inspiration she is bound to a series of paintings as well, greatly increasing the difficulty of the art. All choreographers have found inspiration in painting, but only occasional inspiration, not the idea for an entire work.

In *The Rake's Progress*, to music specially written by Gavin Gordon, de Valois has animated Hogarth's series of narrative pictures, perhaps a still more difficult task. Again she has succeeded in creating a truly English masterpiece. *The Rake's Progress*, while it has not the depth and pathos of the Russian masterpiece, is to English Ballet what *Petrouchka* is to Russian, a truly national expression.

In both these ballets de Valois reveals to an exceptional degree one of the indispensable assets of the choreographer, the ability to produce, an entirely different thing from creation. Production begins when creation has ceased. *The Rake's Progress* is full of interesting characterization brought out in dancing. Even its minor characters, such as the woman with the fan who visits the asylum in the final scene, are complete. There is no *corps de ballet*, but a company of *dancer-actors*. A work of this type is truly English, because the new English dancer, lacking an inherited tradition, excels where she can hide her lack of self-confidence behind a positive role. She has the technique for the classics, but has still to find a full measure of assurance. She can best express herself through the medium of another character. Gavin Gordon's score is an admirable example of well-composed narrative music perfectly suited to its subject.

De Valois tried to animate yet a third picture, Manet's *Bar aux Folies Bergère*, and has failed, for a very positive reason. Success was impossible from the start. Manet is not telling a story. He is not interested in the life of his famous barmaid. What interests him is the solution of the problem of her colour and shape in relation to the bottles on the bar, the red triangle of Bass, the chandelier and the illumination. That problem he has solved, and the solution can have no possible relationship to ballet. It is as absolute as a vase of roses or a

bowl of fruit by the same painter. There can be no question of carrying it a stage farther. The result is that her characters are unconvincing, vaguely reminiscent of another painter, Toulouse-Lautrec, but on the whole more suggestive of the Gay-Paree of the week-end visiting Englishman. No impressionist painter can possibly inspire ballet. The problem of being inspired by another medium, painting, is the same as in the choice of the music. It must be susceptible to *translation*.

XIV. CHECKMATE

Symbolism and realism

Checkmate, designed for the first visit of the Sadler's Wells Ballet to Paris and presented at the Champs Elysées in 1937, is the result of a long and close collaboration so characteristic of the work of Sadler's Wells to-day.

It tells the story of a symbolical game of chess played between Love and Death. The score, by Arthur Bliss, is descriptive and highly dramatic, though in its timing and at intervals in its volume it is conceived on an operatic rather than a balletic principle. De Valois introduces her players in a short scene clearly indicating the nature of the struggle, then the curtain rises on the chessboard and we see the preparations for war. The characters start as completely impersonal beings, very gradually gaining our sympathy as they assume personalities; until we take a vivid interest in the fortunes of the game, siding with the dotard Red King and his loving young wife and with their chivalrous champion Knight against the ruthless Judith-like Black Queen. De Valois has succeeded in conveying not only the tension of the game, but its ultimate importance, alternating hope and despair like a skilled teller of fables in the bazaar.

McKnight Kauffer's décor and costumes are among the most successful in modern ballet. The background shows up the movement, the scene helps to tell the story, the colour scheme echoes the dramatic intensity of the music. In conception the decoration is a skilful compromise between reality and abstraction, just as the dancers are half puppet and half human; a method that suggests vast possibilities in bringing the scenic element back to its partnership in the whole.

XV. FAÇADE

A burlesque

The *suite de danses* known as *Façade*, to music by William Walton, was created for the Camargo Society by Frederick Ashton in 1931. It proved immediately popular, and was taken into the repertoire of the Ballet Club and of Sadler's Wells. It is performed several times every season, and its continued success proves that the humour is not ephemeral.

Façade is a burlesque of dancing in terms of dancing. With extraordinary observation Ashton has seized upon the characteristics of various types of dance and has caricatured them to exactly the same degree that Walton has done in his music. Such a burlesque as apart from satire is a definitely English characteristic, and *Façade* is not an imitation Russian ballet, but a truly original contribution.

There is a tendency to decry all ballet that does not aim deliberately at beauty, and for that reason the merits of so light-hearted a work might easily be overlooked. There is no precedent to suggest that ballet cannot include burlesque, and there are accounts of burlesques in which the Kings of France took part. The burlesque is bad only if it is not 'translated', and *Façade* is yet another striking example of the notion that I explained in the case of *The Three-Cornered Hat*.

The Polka is the most stimulating and original when a classical dancer removes her skirt and performs a ridiculous little dance, but one that at the same time is extremely difficult. One says, in fact, 'all this preparation and all this technique to express that!' and laughs, as one always does at pomposity and anti-climax. The tap-dance and the shooting-dance belong to the humour of a Coward; the Waltz, with its focal point the legs, is a brilliant piece of observation.

XVI. LES PATINEURS: LES RENDEZVOUS

Dancing for the sake of dancing – almost

Each of these ballets of Frederick Ashton's is connected by a slender idea; each one is an admirable success because the medium has been handled with consummate tact.

Les Patineurs is the *translation* of skating in terms of ballet, a burlesque like *Façade*, but one which has as its object the revelation of an astonishing variety of virtuoso technique. To burlesque skating alone might be ingenious, but it would soon become monotonous. While Ashton has been consistent and has never allowed us to forget that the dancers are on ice, he has made each dance technically exciting in itself. Meyerbeer's music is simple, Ashton's action is complex, with the result that we can take it all in at a glance. So skilfully interwoven are his dances, so rapidly do they succeed one another, that what might be a *suite de danses* is actually a ballet. The drama is in the action and not in the idea. The audience asks the question: 'What is going to happen next?' The result is the exceedingly brilliant handling of classicism: dancing for the sake of dancing – almost. And the *almost* gives it a character that makes it acceptable to a modern audience.

Les Rendezvous is also a ballet entirely composed of *arias*. Its theme is brilliantly simple, meetings and partings, and admirably suited to Auber's music. It would be difficult to imagine a theme that could be more directly conveyed in movement or that could link one dance to the next in such logical and rapid succession. Remove the connecting link and the result is a competent commonplace.

AMBROSE

Les Patineurs

In these ballets Ashton challenges the Russians on their own ground, using his dancers with no character disguise.

For both these works William Chappell, a dancer, has devised settings and costumes that are highly effective.

XVII. SYMPHONIC VARIATIONS

A study in pure dancing

The term 'abstract ballet' is a much abused one, as no ballet is purely abstract since all movement is conditioned by music. What is termed abstract ballet is really ballet that is the farthest removed from literature, and that is movement parallel in feeling to music. *Les Sylphides* is a great example of such a work, but *Les Sylphides* is in fact the very essence of romanticism – *Giselle* without a story.

Frederick Ashton's own *Dante Sonata*, while it has no narrative, has an important and powerful theme. His *Symphonic Variations* is a study in pure movement that is parallel in thought to César Franck's music, and is what might be called *visual music*. To attempt such a thing is always risky, especially when the music is familiar, since everyone creates his own visual images. Hence Mr Ashton's triumph in this medium has been all the more complete. A ballet of this type is impossible to describe in words. One would need musical illustration and the presence of a dancer; one must in fact see the ballet itself. This type of work also requires perfect costumes and décor; costumes and décor that suggest nothing concrete. Sophie Fedorovitch, so often Ashton's partner, provided these. Indeed, no work of musical interpretation has been better dressed, and Miss Fedorovitch has avoided the semblance of hygienic underwear so distressing in some of the great symphonic ballets. Her background is completely abstract and so skilfully designed that it fits in with the movement of the dancers and acts, so to speak, as a sounding-board for the music.

Both Frederick Ashton and Sophie Fedorovitch have succeeded in another work in a similar vein – Ravel's *Valses Nobles et Sentimentales*, created for the Sadler's Wells Theatre Ballet. These works call for a very high degree of musicianship from the dancers concerned. They represent the very opposite point of view from Lifar's campaign to make music purely the servant of dancing, which he has put into practice with *Icare* and *Chota Roustaveli*, where composers have supplied rhythm to accompany the choreography. This pure dancing is only safe in the hands of a master choreographer of real musical sensitivity. It does not, any more than the very concrete narratives, present a future trend in ballet.

XVIII. HAMLET

The choreographer as literary critic

This is Robert Helpmann's second ballet, following the successful *Comus*, in which he wedded the masque and the ballet, poetry and the dance, with a considerable measure of success.

Helpmann has taken a literary subject; but as a great 'theatreman' has avoided the many and obvious pitfalls and has remained true to his medium. Others have taken Shakespeare for reasons I have never understood, and have told the stories of the selected plays, usually inadequately. One can only ask oneself: Why? Why? When Shakespeare has done so to perfection! Why? When the story itself is of no importance, when it was already second- or third-hand! When Shakespeare gave it life and beauty!

Helpmann has done nothing of the kind; he has given us the choreographer's comment on Hamlet, a very different matter. He shows us what goes on in Hamlet's mind when, like a drowning man, his life passes in review through his fevered and dying brain. He has shown us this, as he can in his medium, by a series of images that interpret the story according to modern psychology. He does not insist or elaborate, but presents these images dramatically. This is literary criticism perfectly *translated* into ballet, and as such it is an entirely new departure.

One must mention the important role that Leslie Hurry's costumes and décor play in completing the work and making it a whole. They are the link between Tchaikovsky's romanticism and Helpmann's modern viewpoint.

XIX. MIRACLE IN THE GORBALS
Characterization in the round

For a number of reasons this must rank as one of the outstanding creations of contemporary ballet. It dares more than other works; its success is all the greater. The story is the popular one of the return of the Saviour to the modern scene. It is obviously dramatic, but presents many dangers from offensive bad taste to mawkishness. It is a tribute to the success of the ballet that the highest praise has come from the religious press. The setting for this visitation is the Gorbals in Glasgow. This is a singularly happy choice, enabling the choreographer to probe behind the Palais de Danse atmosphere of the crowded city slum on a Saturday night and to find the true emotional depths of these people in their national Scottish dances. Arthur Bliss has written a brilliant score on those lines, making full use of natural sounds, such as the wailing of a ship's siren, and also of Scottish national music. The result is not a sordid slum picture, but a sympathetic study that presents people as they really are, that looks under the surface and can rise to lyrical heights. One of the most moving moments in the whole of ballet occurs when the stranger brings the young suicide to life. At first she still belongs to the world of the spirit, then, gradually, as the blood warms within her, she breaks into some country dance remembered from childhood. The parson who opposes and finally brings about the death of the stranger is no mere villain but a complex personality, capable of great good as well as evil. For the first time this is characterization in the round; these are not puppets but living people. There are two directions that Helpmann might have taken but has not: the impression of a big city, already brilliantly done by Jooss, or the presentation of a social problem, also within the province of Jooss. What he has done is to say, 'Here is a mass of people in a sordid slum. They all look more or less the same. How do they react both as individuals and as a group in a particular emergency?' The ballet is a working out of that, done with great directness but with a subtlety that gradually reveals itself. These tough dwellers in the dockland slum are suddenly moved by the primitive fear of a mountain people when confronted with death.

In this modern miracle play Helpmann, Bliss, and the painter Burra have introduced something new to ballet.

XX. LES FORAINS

A balletic sketch

There is a great difference between a sketchy ballet and a balletic sketch. The balletic sketch is a work of art that is as complete in itself as a drawing by Ingres or Toulouse-Lautrec. The present sketch might be by Picasso in his 'blue' period. It deals with the life of ambulant circus folk, showing the contrast between their penury and their spangled splendour. It is witty, satirical, and infinitely pathetic. The characterization is superb, and once one has seen it one will never forget the hungry little girl with the bird-cage, perched high on the shoulder of the ring-master, or running back at curtain fall to rescue her pigeons.

Bérard's scenery, erected on the stage during the performance, is an integral part of the ballet itself and Sauguet's score completely expresses the daily tragedy of these people.

Les Forains is an outstanding example of French taste in

ballet creation, in which music, choreography, and scenery are completely one.

It is the work of Boris Kochno, most Parisian of Russians, and Diaghileff's right-hand man during the latter period of his life, and the choreography is by that brilliant young French choreographer Roland Petit. Both Kochno and Petit have guided the destinies of Les Ballets des Champs-Elysées, which has meant the direct re-entry of France into ballet creation.

XXI. LE JEUNE HOMME ET LA MORT

A ballet to make your flesh creep

Le Jeune Homme et la Mort has been described by Boris Kochno as the *Le Spectre de la Rose* of our day. Its story is by Jean Cocteau, and the choreography by the brilliantly gifted Roland Petit. It is a perfect study in the decadence of the 1920s. 'A young man is infatuated by a girl who does not return his affections. He pleads with her but she disdainfully refuses his advances and leaves him. In despair the young man hangs himself. The scene changes and Death appears. She takes off her mask and puts it on the young man. Death is the girl who spurns him, but now she leads him forward to happiness.'

The choice of the Passacaglia in C minor by Bach as musical accompaniment to this nightmare may seem incongruous at first. It is shocking, but deliberately so. It enhances the suspense and also, by contrast, the value of the movement employed. Nathalie Philippart and Jean Babilée give performances of great macabre intensity. The choreographer has taken the very best from modern dance technique and this, allied to classical training, is highly effective. The décor by Wakhevitch, with its surprising transformation scene, is in the very best tradition of French decorative art. Kochno knows more about the relationship of décor to ballet than anyone else at the present day. This ballet may be 'ham', it will certainly date and is in doubtful taste, but there can be no doubt of its powerful impact on the audience, or of the skill by which that impact is produced.

It is interesting to note that the ballet was rehearsed entirely to 'swing' music and that the dancers themselves did not hear the Bach until the dress rehearsal. This served to accentuate the contrast between the music and the sordid drama.

XXII. THE GREEN TABLE

A major work outside the Russian tradition

I include one ballet outside the Russian tradition because it is a work of outstanding merit, of continued topical interest, that has been applauded throughout the whole civilized world, the Fascist countries excluded.

Kurt Jooss and his group of dancers from Essen first came into prominence when they won the first prize in the choreographic competition inaugurated by Les Archives Internationales de la Danse. The prize-winning work was *The Green Table*, and though Kurt Jooss has since produced many ballets of considerable merit, he remains the creator of one work, the justification for the existence of the group and for its world travels.

The Green Table is a powerful indictment of the failure of the League of Nations. The curtain rises on an international conference, the senile senators talk, quarrel, shots are exchanged, and then we are shown what happens when Death is let loose. The curtain falls on a repetition of the first act – platitudes, arguments, and shots. Since its creation *The Green Table* has become more and more topical.

Kurt Jooss has evolved a technique of his own, a blend of the Central European methods of Laban with a foundation of ballet technique. His company can boast the most perfect *ensemble* of any to-day – lightness, musicality, and precision.

His fault seems to be his unwillingness to take the fullest advantage of ballet technique. Such a man has the unique opportunity of being able to add much that is valuable to the old system and to use it in new ways. His most expressive scenes in *The Green Table* are the first and last, where the dancers are deliberately limited in movement by their seated positions round the table. Where they are allowed full movement one feels the limitations imposed by his system. Jooss, using ballet technique plus what he has shown us he could add, should be the creator of a series of effective ballets, instead of justly famed as the creator of one great imaginative work.

XXIII. CARMEN AND BALLETIC REALISM

Roland Petit has started by adopting a dangerous principle; he has taken an opera and turned it into ballet. In this particular case there were extenuating circumstances. The opera itself was taken from a short story with a dramatic plot. It is an opera that requires strong acting and perfect characterization, which it rarely receives. If Petit has done violence to the music, and he has treated it admirably on the whole, he has restored Merimée's *Carmen*. It will be difficult in the future to see *Carmen* through other eyes, and this is the measure of his success.

He tells his story in five scenes and with the complete collaboration of the decorative artist, Clavé. The story is naturally a brutal one and it has been treated with realism. Its theme is physical love that turns to hatred through jealousy. The result could easily have been crude and shocking. This would have been so had not Petit made a perfect choreographic translation. The ballet stands by its dancing alone; it is true choreography. The realistic touches are superimposed during production. Petit is both choreographer and producer. Such incidents as the lighting of the cigarette or Don José's wiping of his hands on the curtain underline the reality of the characters. But the passionate *pas de deux* is pure choreography. And the two blend admirably in the same way as the songs and the spoken word do in the opera itself.

The death scene is the most dramatic in contemporary ballet, with its parallel of what is going on in the arena behind and the superb irony of the matador's triumph as the curtain falls on the murdered Carmen and the tormented Don José.

DETAILS OF THE WORKS
COMMENTED ON IN THIS CHAPTER

Giselle: a ballet in two acts by Théophile Gautier and the Chevalier de Saint-Georges after a suggestion by Heine. Choreography by Coralli, music by Adolphe Adam. Created in 1841, with Carlotta Grisi as Giselle. Revived by Diaghileff in 1911 for Karsavina and Nijinsky. Danced by Pavlova, Spessivtseva, Markova, Fonteyn, Chauviré.

The Swan Lake: a ballet in four acts by Tchaikovsky. Choreography by Marius Petipa and Ivanoff. First performed in 1877. Revived in 1894 with Legnani in the leading role. Has been danced by all the leading Russian ballerinas. Revived by Diaghileff in various abbreviated forms, the best known being a one-act version consisting mainly of Act II of the original. Given in full at Covent Garden.

Aurora's Wedding: a one-act abbreviation of *The Sleeping Princess.* Choreography by Petipa, music by Tchaikovsky. The original work given at the Maryinsky in 1890, with Carlotta Brianza as the Princess Aurora, and Cecchetti as the Blue Bird and the Fairy Carabosse. Revived by Diaghileff at the Alhambra in 1921, with Trefilova, Egorova, Spessivtseva, and Lopokova alternating as ballerina. Presented in one act in Paris, 1922. Revived by de Basil in 1935. Revived in full by the Sadler's Wells Company at Covent Garden on February 20th, 1946, with Fonteyn as the Princess.

Les Sylphides: a romantic reverie in one act by Michael

Fokine to music by Chopin. Created as *Chopiniana* for a charity fête in 1908. Presented by Diaghileff the following year. In the repertoire of every ballet company to-day.

Le Spectre de la Rose: choreographic poem in one act by Jean Louis Vaudoyer after a poem by Gautier. Produced by Diaghileff in 1910, with Karsavina and Nijinsky. In every repertoire to-day.

Carnaval: a ballet in one act by Fokine, choreography by Fokine, music by Schumann. Décor and costumes by Bakst. Composed for a charity, then presented by Diaghileff in 1910, with Nijinsky as Harlequin. In every repertoire to-day.

Schéhérazade: a ballet in one act by Michel Fokine. Choreography by Fokine, music by Rimsky-Korsakov, décors and costumes by Bakst. Presented by Diaghileff in 1910. Original cast: Ida Rubinstein as Zobeide, Nijinsky as the Golden Slave. Zobeide subsequently taken by Karsavina. Revived by de Basil, 1935; René Blum, 1936.

Thamar: a ballet in one act by Fokine after Lermontov's poem. Choreography by Fokine, music by Balakirev, décors and costumes by Bakst. Produced in 1912 by Diaghileff. Original cast: Karsavina as Thamar, Bolm as the Prince. Revived by de Basil, 1935.

Prince Igor: the Polovtsian dances to Borodin's opera. Choreography by Fokine, décor and costumes originally by Roerich. Another version by Korovin, presented by Diaghileff in 1909, with Adolph Bolm in the leading role, maintained in the repertoire ever since. Given by de Basil, René Blum, and Léon Woizikowski.

Petrouchka: dance drama in four scenes by Alexandre Benois and Michael Fokine. Choreography by Fokine, music by Stravinsky, décors and costumes by Benois. First presented by Diaghileff in 1911. Original cast: Karsavina, the Dancer; Nijinsky, Petrouchka; Orloff, the Moor. Revived by de Basil, 1922, René Blum, and Léon Woizikowski.

The Three-Cornered Hat: a ballet in one act by Martinez Sierra, after a story by Alarcón. Choreography by Massine, music by de Falla, décor and costumes and drop-curtain by Picasso. Presented by Diaghileff in 1919, with Karsavina and Massine. Revived by de Basil 1934, with Toumanova and Massine. Revived by Sadler's Wells Company at Covent Garden on February 6th, 1947, with Massine and Fonteyn.

La Boutique Fantasque: a ballet in one act, with choreography by Massine, music by Rossini, arranged and orchestrated by Respighi. Décor, costumes, and drop-curtains by Derain. Presented by Diaghileff in 1919, with Lopokova and Massine as the can-can dancers. Revived by de Basil in 1935 with Danilova and Massine. Revived by the Sadler's Wells Company at Covent Garden on February 27th, 1947, with Massine and Shearer as the can-can dancers.

Le Beau Danube: a ballet in one act by Massine. Choreography by Massine, music by Johann Strauss, costumes by Étienne de Beaumont, décor by Polunin after Guys. First produced for Étienne de Beaumont in 1923 with Lopokova, Marra, and Massine. Revived by de Basil in a new form with Danilova, Riabouchinska, and Massine, 1933.

Cotillon: a ballet in one act by Boris Kochno. Choreography by Balanchine, music by Chabrier, décor by Bérard. Produced for de Basil in 1932, with Toumanova, Woizikowski, Lichine, and Rostova.

La Symphonie Fantastique: choreographic symphony in five scenes. Music and theme by Berlioz, choreography by Massine, décor and costumes by Bérard. Produced for de Basil in 1936, with Toumanova as the Beloved, Massine as the Musician.

Job: a masque for dancing in eight scenes by Geoffrey Keynes from the Biblical story. Music by Vaughan Williams, décor and costumes after Blake by G. Raverat, masks by Hedley Briggs. Choreography by Ninette de Valois. Produced for the Camargo Society in 1931, now in Sadler's Wells repertoire. Anton Dolin as Satan; in revivals, Robert Helpmann.

The Rake's Progress: a ballet in six scenes by Gavin Gordon (after Hogarth). Music by Gavin Gordon, choreography by de Valois, décor and costumes by Rex Whistler (after Hogarth). Produced in 1935 with Walter Gore as the Rake, Markova as the Girl. Revived with Robert Helpmann and Elizabeth Miller.

Bar aux Folies Bergère: a one-act ballet by Ninette de Valois. Choreography by de Valois, décor and costumes by William Chappell. Ballet Club production in 1934. Markova as La Goulue.

Checkmate: a ballet in a prologue and one scene by Arthur Bliss. Choreography by Ninette de Valois, décor and costumes by McKnight Kauffer. Produced as Sadler's Wells in 1937 with June Brae as the Black Queen, Pamela May as the Red Queen, Robert Helpmann as the Red King, Harold Turner as the Red Knight. Revived at Covent Garden on November 18th, 1947, Pamela May as the Black Queen, Julia Farron as the Red Queen, Gordon Hamilton as the Red King, Harold Turner as the Red Knight.

Façade: suite de danses in one act by William Walton. Choreography by Frederick Ashton, music by William Walton, décor and costumes by John Armstrong. Camargo Society production in 1931, with Lopokova as the Milkmaid, Markova in the Polka.

Les Patineurs: a ballet in one act with music by Meyerbeer, selected by Constant Lambert. Choreography by Frederick Ashton, décor and costumes by William Chappell. Sadler's Wells, 1937, with Harold Turner, Mary Honer, Elizabeth Miller, June Brae, Pamela May, and Margot Fonteyn.

Les Rendezvous: a ballet in one act with music by Auber (selected by Constant Lambert). Choreography by Ashton, décor and costumes (two versions) by William Chappell. Sadler's Wells, 1935.

Hamlet: music by Tchaikovsky. Décors by Leslie Hurry, choreography by Robert Helpmann. Created at the New Theatre, 1943.

Miracle in the Gorbals: ballet by M. Bentall. Music by Arthur Bliss, décors by Edward Burra, choreography by Robert Helpmann. Created at Prince's Theatre, October 26, 1944.

Symphonic Variations: music by César Franck. Décors by Sophie Fedorovitch, choreography by Frederick Ashton. Created at the Royal Opera House, Covent Garden, April 24, 1946.

Mam'zelle Angot: music by Lecocq. Orchestrated by Gordon Jacob. Décors by Derain, choreography by Leonide Massine. Created at the Royal Opera House, Covent Garden, November 26, 1947.

Les Forains: ballet by Boris Kochno. Music by Sauguet. Décors by Bérard, choreography by Roland Petit. First seen in England at the Adelphi Theatre in the spring of 1946.

Le Jeune Homme et la Mort: ballet by Jean Cocteau. Music by Bach, décors by Wakhevitch, choreography by Roland Petit. First seen in England at the Winter Garden Theatre in the summer of 1947.

Carmen: ballet based on Mérimée's story, music from Bizet's opera, décors and costumes by Clavé, choreography by Roland Petit. Created at Prince's Theatre.

Other important works are discussed under different headings.

CHAPTER EIGHT

Appreciation: Round the World in a Series of Generalizations

I

BALLET has survived wars and revolutions, changes of fashion and long journeys to new continents. The quality of its technique has remained unchanged, its aesthetic has not greatly altered since Noverre wrote his letters. It is an art of tradition obstinate in its will to survive. It has in its comparatively short life appealed to kings and their courtiers, to aesthetes and to the masses. Yet in spite of this stability of basic technique and aesthetics, no art changes its leading figures with greater frequency; a balletic generation lasts some fifteen years.

I am going to give a few generalizations on the development of the last fifteen years; the scene is still too fluid to do more than that.

(A) Throughout the world ballet has become more popular and has tapped a vast new public.

(B) The ambulant *ballet russe* (Diaghileff model) has no longer any creative vitality, largely owing to economic circumstances.

(C) Ballet has become national. England, France, and the United States have taken Russian Ballet and adapted it to their physical, temperamental, and aesthetic needs.

These are the three vital changes that have taken place. They have their advantages and their grave dangers.

The advantages lie in the new blood brought to an old art that might have suffered from inbreeding. The danger comes from the smug academism that always threatens subsidized enterprises and from tendencies of artistic chauvinism. A travelling company directed by a real artist can afford (or could afford) shock tactics that make the more intelligent pause and take stock. *Parade* or *Le Jeune Homme et la Mort* could never have been produced on an opera-house stage. Finally, excessive popularity lowers standards. *The Red Shoes* is a case in point. It may turn a vast new public to ballet, but that public will be looking for stars and not for the fourfold art of ballet.

Let us now see how various nations and their companies are dealing with the situation.

II. GREAT BRITAIN

If I start with Great Britain it is not for any patriotic reason, but because here the growing process is complete and the pattern clear.

There are four main reasons for the high standard of our ballet; the wise leadership of Ninette de Valois, the conception of an Arts Council by Lord Keynes, the natural discipline of the English with its team spirit, and the fact that having no local tradition we could go direct to the great tradition of ballet.

I wrote at the beginning of this chapter that *ballet russe* was adapting itself to national needs. It was an easy and an obvious thing to write, but it is not so easy to give concrete examples without coming down to those anecdotal generalizations about Englishmen, Frenchmen, Russians, and Elephants.

How has England used the ballet?

In England ballet is in the hands of dancers and the focus is on classicism. My reader may not unnaturally ask at this point: 'But isn't ballet always in the hands (or the feet) of the dancers? If not, who can control it?'

The answer is that during the romantic era it was the poet, Théophile Gautier largely, who used ballet as a medium, and in the Diaghileff era it was the aesthetician, Diaghileff himself, the poet Cocteau, the painter Picasso, who used the medium. In the second, the Diaghileff period, the choreographer was more important than in the first, but he was only one-fourth of the ballet-creation team. In England to-day he is the leader and at times the whole. Therefore our record in decorative art is unimpressive, very few original scores have been commissioned for ballet – Bliss is a magnificent exception – and the poet has not had a look in at all. Yet undoubtedly the Sitwells, Christopher Fry, and others have a great contribution to make.

On the other hand our record in choreography and dancing is outstanding. This is a far healthier tendency than the reverse. We have the varied work of Ashton, de Valois, and Helpmann, Andrée Howard, John Cranko, Alfred Rodrigues and others, and a repertoire enriched from outside by the Petipa-Ivanoff classics, by Fokine, Massine, Balanchine, and Petit. We have never made the mistake of parish-pumpery.

The Dominions share England's love of ballet and are producing magnificent material. Indeed, our own ballet might well be called a Commonwealth Ballet. This means that the Dominions seem to be handicapped in their attempts to form national companies by the fact that talent automatically makes its way to London. A long-term view, and that is essential in ballet, will show that far from being a handicap this will prove of the greatest advantage. The Commonwealth dancer will gain an experience only possible in a large city through performing in front of a cosmopolitan audience and critics with a world standard. Then gradually, for one reason or another, dancers will return to their native countries really well equipped to form part of a national ballet.

III. FRANCE

France, like England, has a contemporary ballet that is directly descended from Diaghileff; in our case, through de Valois and

Rambert; in that of France, through Lifar and Kochno. But France differs from us in the important particular that it had an old tradition, the most venerable of all, that had grown completely stagnant, when the French Petipa brought his genius to Russia. In any study of French ballet that must always be borne in mind.

Let me attempt a generalization of the French scene: it is either that or a complete book.

(i) Ballet is as much the concern of poets, painters, and musicians as of dancers and choreographers.

(ii) The French character tends to extreme individualism; the star is brilliant, the corps de ballet weak.

(iii) The French enjoy novelty, especially the novelty that expresses current artistic thought. The classics are neglected, except those portions that allow the individual to shine.

IV. THE UNITED STATES

Ballet in the United States is also an offshoot of *ballet russe*, but in a different way. There was no local tradition, and indeed no strong ballet tradition at all apart from the visits of Elssler and Pavlova. Diaghileff was almost unknown, though Nijinsky the star had been seen. Russian dancers, including Fokine, Bolm, and Mordkin, had settled in America as teachers, but beyond planting a technique they had been unable to spread the belief that ballet was an art form. It was in fact highly suspect, and only the American modern dance had virtue. The visits of de Basil in 1933-4 changed the situation. It was George Balanchine and the critic, Lincoln Kirstein, who, with the founding of the American School of Ballet (1934), planted a sound tradition that has grown and developed.

Here once again is a generalization:

(i) America brings all the excitement of a discovery of ballet, great vitality and interest in technical virtuosity for its own sake, a magnificent physique, rhythm.

(ii) **Two** opposing schools of choreography: the neo-classicism of Balanchine, storyless and eurhythmic, a classicism for a new tradition, and the Americana of *Rodeo* (de Mille), *Fall River Legend* (de Mille), *Fancy Free* (Robbins), a *ballet folklorique* for a new tradition.

There are also the ballets of Anthony Tudor, creations that belong to no particular school, though his greatest work, *Pillar of Fire*, is inspired by the American scene.

The New York City Ballet specializes in Mr Balanchine's ballets, Ballet Theater in Americana.

Apart from her native-born dancers America has absorbed many of the Russians, most prominent amongst them Tamara Toumanova – for some time an étoile at the Paris Opéra – Igor Yusskevitch, André Eglevsky, and George Skibine.

The South American republics, with their magnificent opera-houses, have been forming companies often under the guidance of former de Basil dancers. It is too early to say with what results, or whether the somewhat involved political relations that so often exist will allow stability and consequent artistic development.

V. DENMARK

The Danish Royal Ballet would have been dealt with immediately after French Ballet had this been an historical survey. The school has a tradition of close on two hundred years, and is active at the present day. It is perhaps the oldest surviving style of ballet. Its aesthetic comes directly from Auguste Bournonville (1805–79), the son of Antoine Bournonville (1760–1843), the French dancer and choreographer pupil of Noverre, who succeeded the Italian Galeotti as guiding spirit of the Danish Ballet. In a sense, Auguste Bournonville is still guiding the Danish Ballet, where a French style of a great but quaint charm survives, one that is to-day quite unknown in France.

Moreover, the Danish Ballet is rich in its possession of such Bournonville classics as *Napoli*. Denmark seems faced with the difficult problem of whether to attempt to bring her ballet up to date with that of the other ballet countries, both in choreography and school, or to remain as a treasure-house of the past, a charming and picturesque backwater off the main stream of ballet.

This is less of a problem than it appears. It is, in fact, not a problem at all. Russia, too, has a similar tradition, and a closely related school through Johannsen, who was a pupil of Bournonville's. Johannsen was the teacher of the great generation of Russian ballerinas that included Pavlova. By learning a more general and extended technique, the Danes would not lose their Bournonville style; this lies in the choreography and not in the classroom. In other words, a Pavlova in the past or a Markova, Chauviré, or Fonteyn to-day could, with careful rehearsal, perform a Bournonville classic; it is doubtful whether a dancer trained purely in Bournonville terms could shine in *Swan Lake* or *Les Sylphides*. There is no such thing as Petipa training or Fokine training, even though the two styles are so different. True classical training should embrace Petipa, Fokine, Balanchine, and Roland Petit – and Bournonville.

Also, making a fetish of this Bournonville manner, they have stressed male dancing at the expense of the women; which Bournonville himself must have done as dancer-choreographer. The young Danish women in the company and in the school are as fine material as anywhere, but they are, as yet, given insufficient chance to develop. There is no real stress on youth and the future, only on the traditional performance of a limited repertoire. The traditional soon becomes purely academic and sterile. Though not an expert on this period, I would be surprised if it had not already picked up certain mannerisms.

I stress these dangers because they must be faced, but there is a strong chance that Denmark may take a leading place among the chief ballet nations (and not merely because of the historic interest of the repertoire). Vera Volkova is now in charge of the company classes, and Volkova, apart from her exceptional skill as a teacher, was a pupil of Vaganova, who was the pupil of Johannsen. There is an opportunity, therefore, of a broadening of technique that need not frighten the most ardent diehard; and there seem to be as many blimps as there were in St Petersburg in the days of Petipa.

I have mentioned few dancers by name for reasons stated. I cannot, however, omit Gerda Karstens, one of the most outstanding character mimes I have ever seen, or Erik Bruhn, a male dancer of true nobility as well as a brilliant teacher of children. Here are guides for the future.

VI. RUSSIA

Russia apart, we have almost covered the ballet-conscious countries.

It is difficult to write of a country where the arts are so much at the service of politics that it is rare to find an impartial opinion. Of Russia one can only say for sure that (*a*) the natural talent of the Russian for ballet and his love of the art remain unimpaired; (*b*) the school is the same that produced Trefilova, Pavlova, and Karsavina; Ulanova is in that great tradition; (*c*) in presentation as apart from technique the dancer is inclined to be a little too obvious in projection, since the ballet public is so much less sophisticated than in the past (where a company does not travel and allow itself to be criticized there must be certain provincialisms); (*d*) decoratively and dramatically, ballet in Russia is still in the pre-Diaghileff phase. Lavish and somewhat unsophisticated spectacle is the most appreciated. In the Workers' Russia as in the Tsar's Russia, a fountain of real water on the stage causes the greatest pleasure; (*e*) choreography is being constantly enriched by the almost endless source of folk material available, all of which has been carefully nursed by the present régime.

VII. AND THE REST

Yugoslavia: Yugoslavia has definitely a great contribution to make to ballet. Her people are natural dancers, her folk material exceptionally rich, and the necessary organization exists, especially in Belgrade. It is now a matter of finding the right teachers and of time before a Yugoslav ballet takes a prominent place in the theatre.

Turkey: Turkey has started in the right way, with a school opened under the guidance of Dame Ninette de Valois. After the first 'dance generation' the results should be striking.

Italy: Ballet the very poor relation of opera – misunderstood and usually maltreated.

Greece: Every dancer a concert soloist who is all too often guilty of un-Greek activities in imitating Greek sculpture on historic sites; a malady that I only believed existed in the English suburbs and the American college campus.

Germany: The Germans are inclined to look for a philosophy of the dance, a dangerous attitude when perhaps the soundest philosophy is Gautier's, 'I love ballet because it makes me forget the drabness of the present fashions.' The young people, however, are beginning to relish ballet and to talk of Wigmanism and Labanism as 'the old-fashioned dance'. The problem once again will be to find the right teachers.

Austria: Johann Strauss, together with Viennese charm, is regarded as an admirable substitute for a too rigorous school.

If there are any countries where there is no worth-while ballet activity I can only rejoice that some places remain that will afford me a perfect holiday. I only state it here for the sake of the record and not by way of censure.

CHAPTER NINE

What Do They Know of Ballet . . .?

I

In the chapter on the Historical Background of Ballet I wrote, *The history of ballet is but a fragment of the history of dancing.* This is worth stressing from many points of view, not least of all the purely practical. All dancing is potential ballet material, in the present and future as it was in the past. To exclude those outside influences either from prejudice or ignorance would mean eventually to kill ballet from a deficiency disease. Fortunately to-day there is an increasing public for forms of dancing outside ballet.

The ballet being directly composed for an audience is comparatively easy to explain to an audience. Is there any sense or purpose in attempting to explain other forms of dance in a book that is intended to be a practical guide? Is it possible for me to write anything about the various techniques of Indian or Spanish dancing that will add to my readers' pleasure and knowledge? Have they anything in common?

I believe that it is possible at any rate to clear the ground and to underline some of the problems. Also I have no doubt that all dance forms have so much in common that it is possible for anyone with experience in one branch of dancing to distinguish the exceptional dancer, even without a close knowledge of his particular technique. An expert in one school of sculpture is not blind to all other schools.

There are three main reasons for dancing, apart from spontaneous movements of joy or sorrow:

(*a*) For purposes of magic or religion.
(*b*) For social reasons, recreation, or courtship.

(*c*) For an audience.

Now, these three distinct forms of dance are by no means in watertight compartments. The magic or ritual dance may be performed for sheer pleasure hundreds of years after the reason for its performance has been forgotten. It goes on being danced for purely social reasons. The social dance may gain in complexity until only those who have undergone a long and specialized training can undertake it. It is then danced for an audience. This not only gave birth to ballet, but is happening every day in front of us, when the Palais-de-Danse champions become so highly proficient (and so solemn) that they turn professional.

The two most familiar non-balletic dance forms seen in our theatres are Spanish and Indian. They have this in common – each one is in the difficult transition stage from (*a*) and (*b*) into (*c*). It is of great practical importance for us, if we are critically inclined, and for the dancers to allow for that fact, for it will greatly affect our pleasure.

II. SPANISH DANCING

The Spanish dance that we see is, with the exception of the classical *Bolero*, not primarily designed for the stage. It is partly a social country dance and partly a gipsy entertainment that takes place in cave or tavern in an intimate relationship with the audience. Quite clearly then, as far as the stage is concerned, this is raw material. The producer is faced with the serious problem of refining it or translating it for the stage. This explains much that we see and that may irritate us. It is important to know when and why to stifle or to direct criticism.

(i) The continual rise and fall of the curtain as unrelated item follows unrelated item.

(ii) The peasant dance that is given a comic character instead of being danced straight. These peasants are always made into rustic buffoons, both stupid and coy, and the whole thing is embarrassing.

(iii) The gipsy dance set in a tavern scene with a company audience taking our place round the dancers, drinking imaginary wine and egging them on.

(iv) The musical poverty of many of the items, as a not too good theatre orchestra takes the place of the peasant musicians.

These have become the conventions of Spanish dance shows, in Spain just as much as on tour. They could be overcome, but possibly at too great a loss in view of the particular character of Spanish dancing. The Russian Ballet working with Spanish artists showed us a perfect theatrical translation in *The Three-Cornered Hat*. It is a great ballet, it is a great Spanish ballet, but it does *not* give one the very essence of Spanish dancing. The refining process has been too complete for that.

The very essence of Spanish dancing is individuality, something that is the complete opposite of the *corps de ballet*, something also that rebels against dancing to music carefully orchestrated and of set tempo. The guitarist follows the dancer's moods, while the dancer inspires the guitarist in a relationship that is exciting and unique. Every performance is a creation, and therefore an improvisation. To stress the theatre side, with its orders and its disciplined cues, is to stifle that sense of creation.

The Spanish dance has its rich techniques that are exciting in themselves, but in no other form of dancing that I know is technique in the narrow sense less important. I have seen a monstrously fat and elderly dancer seated on a stool and just moving her arms and wrists to the rhythm of the music. It cannot be described, it was little more than a beating of time. It was complete, it was expressive; sad, then gay, alluring, and always aristocratic. There was not an ounce of technique except from the point of view of stagecraft, but there was magic. Magic to that degree is rare, but there are many Spanish dancers, who can only perform a very few steps, capable of thrilling an audience. It does not matter whether the audience understands or not; for that matter, there is absolutely nothing to understand but there is everything to feel. These thrills may be sandwiched between much that is vulgar in presentation and much that is boring. To return home and criticize these performances is easy; everything that we have seen, with the exception of fragments from Pilar Lopez, Mariemma, and José Greco, can be pulled to pieces by the man of taste.

My practical advice, therefore, is to understand the background of these performances and the problems involved, and to realize that if the performer can thrill you even for a moment or two, you have had wonderful good fortune.

Just one word more. Spanish dancing is far richer than is usually imagined, and flamenco dancing is but one branch of it. Note the difference between the *zapateado* and a tap-dance. What a world apart. But of whatever kind it is it has dignity and even a certain restraint in the sense that the truly great dancer, however strong the impact he makes, always gives one the feeling of very great power held in reserve. Its dignity lies in the wonderfully erect carriage of the body. If a dancer wriggles, as we so often see in the chorus of *Carmen*, it is quite certain that she is not Spanish. There are a number of Spanish dancers from South Kensington and Bayswater.

III. INDIAN DANCING

The Indian dance faces some of the same problems, and others that to a Western audience are far more complicated. It was originally designed for ritual purposes, probably as a danced illustration of the Rig Vedic Hymns. It is therefore helpful to have some knowledge of the meaning of the gestures, especially as the Westerner can gain no help from the music. It is worth mentioning that it is only quite recently that the

Indian dance has been rediscovered and purified by the Indians themselves. One must not therefore imagine that because one has an Indian friend he can understand and explain the Indian dance. It may be just as much a mystery to him as the *Rose Adagio* to someone who has never been near ballet, and a greater proportion of Indians are unfamiliar with their dancing than the English with ballet. There are four main techniques that are usually given in a programme.

Bharata Natyam, the oldest known surviving dance form said to date from 1500 B.C., though it was only written about in A.D. 1000. This is a pure temple dance found in and around Madras, and varies from steps of pure dance to hymns and songs of praise with a definite meaning. To the Westerner this is the most austere and classical school, yet within a very short time it is possible to feel its particular logic and the extraordinary knowledge of anatomy upon which it is based. It is possible to enjoy it from a purely abstract point of view, and then gradually to feel it; indeed, to feel it so strongly that a false movement would cause an almost physical jar. The only fatal bar to enjoyment would be to ask oneself sentence by sentence what it all meant.

If, as is obvious, we are handicapped by the music, the Indian dance has the advantage of costumes that are perhaps the most beautiful yet devised; the costumes that reveal the grace of the tanagra figure and that are coloured as brightly as the tanagra once was. How much nearer to Greece are these dancers than the white-sheeted young women who perform what they imagine to be the Greek dance. Perfect in line, glowing and brilliant, yet never clashing in colour however daring the combination may seem, they are sufficient in themselves to hold our delighted attention. And we only realize their true nature when we think of the East as devised by the Westerner, whether it be the exotic genius of a Bakst or the garish vulgarity of the Oriental bazaar on ice.

The Kathakali Dance of Malabar is the most exciting, telling in mime and dance the stories of gods and heroes. It is the Hindu equivalent of the Mystery Play. Even when the legends are unfamiliar the atmosphere is clearly conveyed, for we immediately recognize that we are in the presence of gods and heroes, whose quarrels can rock the earth. This is tremendous drama. I have seen it transport one from the dusty boards of a parish-hall platform to the Hindu Olympus, wherever that may be.

The Kathak Dance is greatly influenced by the Moslems, and gives one the impression of a living series of Persian minia-tures. It is used as entertainment, and therefore both in tech-nique and expression it is far more accessible to the Westerner.

The Manipuri Dance seems to me among the most graceful and the most feminine of all dance forms. I use the word graceful in our Western sense. It is certainly the least highly technical. It is the form that Tagore used in his renaissance of the Indian dance.

This, then, represents an exceptionally rich language of the dance that could and has been translated by Ram Gopal, Mrinalini Sarabhai, and others into terms of dance drama for the theatre. The tyro must enjoy it in exactly the same way as he enjoys any of the variations in a Petipa ballet: that is without asking what every movement means. Above all, he must not worry about the word *authentic* that he will most certainly hear used in the interval, usually by those self-acknowledged experts who dabble in Yoga and imagine that every Hindu is spiritual.

If authentic means exactly the same dancing as one would see during a trip to India, then nothing that we have seen in Western Europe is authentic; and I would say fortunately so. In India a performance may last a whole night, a solo dance two or three hours! What we are seeing is something that has been selected for us and, perhaps, translated into terms of the

Western stage, where an audience is seated in front and not all around the performers. The word authentic does not mean a facsimile. The only sense in which it means anything is whether it is authentic in spirit.

I remember remonstrating with an Indian dancer because an ugly microphone stood out in front of the highly decorative band of musicians. He defended it on the grounds that it was authentic in that it was now always done in India. I still maintain that I was right; with the microphone the West came on to the stage and swamped the East. In any case, a microphone does not belong on the stage either in *Swan Lake* or Kathakali (or, for that matter, in the music-hall, where it has killed the comic and substituted the crooner).

The next twenty-five years will see an extraordinary development in the use and understanding of the Indian dance, and a greater public than it has ever known in the West. It is just reaching the end of the transition period between theatre and the surroundings of its birth.

IV. THE CONCERT DANCER

In England, the most dance-loving country, there is no public for the concert dancer; while in America there are nearly as many as there are singers and pianists. Are we neglecting something of value? Is there a possible comparison between concert dancer and *leider* singer, in the sense that the ballet dancer and the opera singer are opposite numbers?

There is, of course, no basis for comparison. The concert singer is interpreting the songs of great composers. She does not pretend to be a theatrical artist. The concert dancer interprets works of her own creation, using a technique of her own devising. And there is no such thing as an accepted modern technique in the sense that there is a Spanish technique or a ballet technique. The non-ballet dancer (I call her a 'modern' dancer though the form seems to me extremely old fashioned) uses a technique mainly devised for her own particular physique. She needs a stage as a background, yet her work does not belong to the theatre. Finally, there is the all-important time factor – a solo dance of over two minutes is a very long one. I suggest to ballet-goers that they time some of the more famous variations. The result will astonish them. If they have ever watched one of these ghastly ballet competitions, they will see how long a one-minute dance can seem. I once heard someone ask Pavlova why she troubled to have a company, since her solos had the greatest success. She replied that she would consider it impudence to try to hold an audience the whole evening on her own.

These reasons show that the instinct of the English public is sound, that, genius apart, there is no justification for the concert dancer, and that in most cases she is a dilettante who could not make her presence felt in competition with others. That was certainly the case with the many Central European or 'modern' dancers who performed in the 1920s. They exploited literary ideas, usually of a morbid type. They could never do anything light or gay; the stock subjects were Death, Lunacy, Famine, Witchcraft, War. Often they were amusing, but seldom by design.

Rules and reason, however, can always be upset by genius or exceptional personality. It happened in the case of Isadora Duncan. It may possibly happen again.

V. THE AFRICAN DANCE

One of the most spontaneous forms of dancing known is that of the American Negro. Watch a coloured and a white dancer, however good, performing a tap-dance, and it is an entirely different thing. The African's tap-dance is often artless, but the white man's tap-dance is not art unless it is embellished by an Astaire or a Paul Draper.

Of recent years the Negro dance has been developed as a

definite art form. It has reached down to roots far deeper than the Southern plantation. The anthropologist has taken a hand, doing consciously what in Europe happened by chance and over a long period. Katherine Dunham, a remarkable woman who has made a major contribution to the dance, an artist and scientist combined, has solved this problem of translation of raw material into terms of theatre. She has solved it so brilliantly and with such apparent ease that it took our public quite a considerable time to realize that they were watching something very much deeper than just a popular 'coloured' show. Paris found that out after the first night.

Dunham went to Africa and the Caribbean for her sources, but she realized that she could only exploit her material by using a disciplined technique. This she did by taking exactly what she needed from ballet and combining it with more primitive movement. She gave her dancers a musical as well as a rhythmic training. Whether popularity damages her work or high expenses prevent its development, both alas possibilities, Katherine Dunham is one of the very few in the recent history of the dance to have developed a new technique.

Illustrated Glossary of some Common Terms

Adagio signifies the 'high spot' of the ballet, when the ballerina, assisted by her partner, displays her grace and virtuosity. It is the *aria* of opera. It is a slow movement stressing balance.

Arabesque. There are a number of different *arabesques*. Basically it is the position of the body on one leg with the other extended behind, one arm in front and the other behind, forming the longest line that can be made from finger-tips to toes. The graceful, sweeping line along the back contrasts with, and is accentuated by, the angle formed by the legs. (See illustration above.)

Attack. The method of presentation, the deliberation behind the performance of the steps.

Attitude. Carlo Blasis finished a pirouette in the pose of Gian Bologna's famous Mercury. There are a number of possible attitudes. (See illustration on right.)

Balletomane is a word first used in Russia to signify the man who never missed a single performance, sitting in the front-row seats, which were almost impossible to obtain without good fortune or influence, being often handed down from father to son. The balletomane was usually a staunch conservative and a fierce partisan. After the performance he would adjourn to a café, meet the dancers, and discuss the ballets until the early hours. He was as mad as anyone with a hobby, but well-informed, a mime of history and tradition, and a connoisseur of technique.

To-day the word might be translated by 'ballet fan'. Anyone who visits the ballet a few times and knows a dancer calls himself a balletomane. There are also near-lunatics with all the enthusiasm but little of the knowledge of the Russian balletomane, who cause a certain amount of damage and a great deal of merriment. The present writer was responsible for loosing the word on the English language and for coining *balletomania* to describe the particular disease, and has suffered for it in many ways, but has no wish to be cured.

Barre. A rod running round the walls of a dance-studio which the pupils hold during their first exercises and while they are being placed. It steadies them, taking the place of the partner's hand.

Centre Practice. The second half of the ballet class, in which the *barre* is not used for support.

Divertissement. An entertainment made up of a series of disconnected dances, usually a hopeless muddle; cf. *suite de dances.*

Elevation. Dancing in the air, *la grâce sautée*, as opposed to *terre-à-terre* dancing. Elevation came in with the shortening of the skirts. The importance is not merely the height reached – this must depend on the time allowed by the music – but the gentleness of the landing. A loud thud will destroy all illusion of flying.

Enchaînement is the sequence of steps; a phrase in the poem that is a dance.

Entrechat. A jump during which the feet change their position with regard to one another four, six, eight times, and, as a freak stunt, ten. (See illustration below.)

Five Positions. The basic positions of the feet from which all movements start and in which all movements end. (See illustration below.)

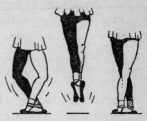

The arms and the head also have their positions.

Fouetté. Without qualification this means a turn on one leg, accompanied by a whipping motion of the other. A trick that is popular and often acquired by those with no knowledge of dancing, though

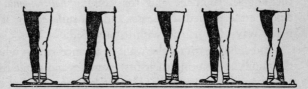

to many it seems the ultimate aim. Many recent ballets call for multiple *fouettés.* (See illustration below.)

Movements in Dancing. There are seven types of movement: *Plier* (to bend), *Étendre* (to stretch), *Relever* (to raise), *Glisser* (to slide), *Sauter* (to jump), *Élancer* (to dart), *Tourner* (to turn).

Pas. A step of which there is an infinite variety, which may either be slid, beaten, turned, or jumped.

They have such attractive names as : *Assemblés, Coupés, Gargouillades, Pas de Chat, Pas de Cheval,* etc., etc., that are descriptive either of their type or origin. I have here described the more obvious ones, *Entrechat*, *Fouetté*, and *Pas de Bourrée*.

The spectator will soon learn to identify them; if he doesn't, no matter; but he must never let the fascination of technique occupy too great a role in his interests. The dancer must learn them until they are second nature and can be rendered expressively.

Pas de Bourrée. Progression on the points by a sequence of very small, even steps; one of the most beautiful effects in ballet, suggestive of gliding. *The Dying Swan* is largely composed of the *pas de bourrée*.

Pirouette. A complete turn of the body accomplished on one leg. There are a variety of pirouettes.

Rond de Jambes. (See illustration.)

Suite de Danses. A series of dances connected by mood and music, but not by theme, e.g. *Aurora's Wedding*, *Les Sylphides*, *Cimarosiana*, *Façade*.

Sur les Pointes. On the tips of the toes; an incident in ballet, used either to give an illusion of flight or of conquest over weight or to facilitate turns by lessening the resistance. Was first introduced, so far as we know, at the time of Taglioni. Only one part of ballet technique, under normal circumstances neither difficult nor painful to acquire. In many cases it comes naturally: to Cossacks, for instance, who can rise on their points without blocked shoes. Certain shoes contain metal blocks, but apart from the noise these make, they are clumsy and unnecessary. Most dancers darn the tips of their shoes to get a better grip of the floor and for economy's sake. Never use toe-dancing as the equivalent of ballet dancing: it is entirely inaccurate. Ballet dancing existed before the use of points, and exists without their use.

The foot can be *à terre* (on the ground), *à quart* (heel slightly off the ground), *sur la demi-pointe*, *à trois quarts*.

Tour en l'Air. A complete aerial turn of the body.

Index

Index

207

Index

Index

PENGUIN BOOKS

━━━━━━━

*The following pages describe
books of various kinds published
by Penguin Books in the
different Penguin and Pelican
series. A complete list is
available on application*

━━━━━━━

PELICAN BOOKS

The Jacaranda Tree – H. E. Bates

A powerful novel and to quote George Malcolm Thomson, 'the lavish and cruel beauty of Burma is transmitted from Bates' remarkable memory to the reader's mind'. (1034)*

Herself Surprised – Joyce Cary

'There seems to me more truth of human nature, a profounder understanding of the springs of action in *Herself Surprised* than in any novel I have read for a long time.' L. P. Hartley in *The Sketch*. (1033)*

The Headmistress – Angela Thirkell

Readers will again thank Mrs Thirkell for the sparkle and humanity of a delightful story, and for introducing them to still more of her engaging characters. (1039)*

Holy Deadlock – A. P. Herbert

This entertaining novel has more to recommend it than most books of its kind, because it helped to change the law of the land. It helped to get the author's divorce reform Bill passed in Parliament. (1038)†

Memoirs of a Midget – Walter de la Mare

A novel by the famous poet, of which Rebecca West said in *The New Statesman*, 'For centuries to come this book will inspire imaginative people'. (1044)*

2s 6d each

* NOT FOR SALE IN THE U.S.A.

† NOT FOR SALE IN THE U.S.A. OR CANADA

A Short History of Confucian Philosophy – Wu-Chi Liu

A book for the general reader who wants to know at first hand about China's greatest philosophy, which has moulded the Chinese nation for almost twenty-five centuries. (A 333)   2s

Man on his Nature – Sir Charles Sherrington

An invigorating expression of a biologist's philosophy, described by *The Sunday Times* as 'one of the landmarks in the history of man's speculation'. (A 322)†   2s 6d

Man, Morals and Society – J. C. Flugel

'Those who wish to know what psycho-analysis has to say on fundamental moral problems will here find an exposition written with great clarity and candour, based on a thorough grasp of all the relevant data and likely to stimulate further inquiry.' *The Spectator*. (A 324)*   3s 6d

The Colour Problem – A. H. Richmond

A study of colour prejudice, racial discrimination, and social separation, with an account of racial relations and the 'colour-bar' in Britain and Commonwealth territories in Africa and the West Indies. (A 328)   3s 6d

Sex and Society – Kenneth Walker and Peter Fletcher

The psychological and social implications of various topics related to sex are here discussed in the belief that human sexuality is more than an autonomous function and involves the whole personality. (A 332)   2s

* NOT FOR SALE IN THE U.S.A.

† NOT FOR SALE IN THE U.S.A OR CANADA

Animal Painting in England – Basil Taylor

This survey from Barlow to Landseer has seventy plates, of which six are in colour, an introductory essay, biographies of the artists, notes on the plates, and a bibliography. (A 251)   3s 6d

Bird Recognition 3 – James Fisher

The third volume in this series, describing the appearance, life, and habits of the rails, game-birds, and larger perching and singing birds, with many maps and charts and nearly seventy illustrations by 'Fish-Hawk'. (A 177)   3s 6d

Electricity – Eric de Ville

Its discovery, the landmarks of its history, its use and modern developments are clearly explained with the aid of 16 pages of plates and many line drawings in the text. (A 323)   2s

Microbes and Us – Hugh Nicol

This book draws attention to the fact that man must either go on offering oblations of fossil fuel to the inhabitants of the soil, or suffer the consequences. (A 326)   2s 6d

Porcelain through the Ages – George Savage

A survey of the main porcelain factories of Europe and Asia with 64 pages of plates, many line drawings, a bibliography, and tables of makers' marks. (A 298)   5s

Contemporary British Art

The aim of this Pelican Book is to give a survey of British painting and sculpture at mid century. The text attempts to isolate and account for a specifically British element in the general confusion of styles, and to trace significant movements and groupings. The leading artists of the modern school are dealt with, and their influence on their younger contemporaries is estimated. The seventy plates, six of which are in colour, illustrate the work of as many artists, and these, together with the accompanying biographical notes, make the volume the most convenient and comprehensive guide to the subject yet published. (A 250)

The Meaning of Art

When this book first appeared it was described in the *Star* as 'the best pocket introduction to the understanding of art that has ever been published', a verdict endorsed by the fact that it had gone through five impressions before Sir Herbert Read made extensive revisions and additions for this Pelican edition. In this lucid discussion he endeavours to provide a basis for the appreciation of pictures and sculpture by defining the elements which go to their making.

A large part of the book is devoted to a compact survey of the world's art, from primitive cave-drawings to Salvador Dali, an exposition designed to show the persistence of certain principles and aspirations throughout the history of art, and to summarize the essence of such movements as Gothic, Baroque, Impressionism, Surrealism. ... It is illustrated by 66 half-tones and 3 line drawings. (A 213) *

3s 6d each

* NOT FOR SALE IN THE U.S.A.

An Outline of European Architecture
NIKOLAUS PEVSNER

This is a history of Western architecture as an expression of Western civilization described historically in its growth from the ninth to the twentieth century. It does not deal with the architecture of classical antiquity, or, generally, with that of the first thousand years A.D. With these exceptions, it tells the story of Western and Central European architecture during the last thousand years through the medium of its outstanding expressions in actual building. Not every architect or every work of importance is mentioned; but the styles discussed and the points raised are illustrated by descriptions of individual buildings which exemplify them. The method adopted is to discuss a few buildings of each period and country in some detail and to avoid dull cataloguing. The aim of the book is to make readers appreciate architectural values. It is written for reading, not merely for reference, and it makes interesting reading indeed in its concentration and its combination of warmth and scholarship. (A 109)   3s 6d

An Introduction to Modern Architecture
J. M. RICHARDS

An Introduction to Modern Architecture, which was first published in 1940, but has now been revised and brought up to date, sets out to explain what 'modern' architecture is all about. In these days, when the need for new buildings is so great and so many building plans are being made, it is specially important that everyone should have an understanding of the principles of architecture, and the author, disapproving of the treatment of architecture as a professional mystery or merely a matter of correct taste, asks (and tries to answer) the simple question: 'Conventions and habits apart, what sort of architecture does our time really require?'
(A 61)   2s 6d

The Pelican History of Art

Edited by Nikolaus Pevsner
Slade Professor of Fine Art in the University of Cambridge

Each volume has about 300 text pages and about
190 pages of half-tone illustrations

THE PENGUIN SCORES

This series has been planned to meet the needs of concert-goers who wish to follow orchestral performances with a pocket score. The majority of volumes are oblong, and slightly larger than a standard Penguin. Each volume has a musical introduction and a biographical note preceding the score. The editor is Professor Gordon Jacob.

THE SYMPHONY

Edited by Ralph Hill

This volume devoted to the symphonies of the great composers is addressed to serious students of music, students who *think* about music as well as *listen* to it, and do not merely approach music sensuously, like a hot bath or a pipe of tobacco. We grant that the sensuous appeal of music is a vital and important part of appreciation, but it is only a part and not the whole. Our first reaction to music is an emotional one, after which, if we are intelligent listeners, we want to know something about its construction, how the composer obtains this or that effect, and the process of his thought. The purpose of this book is, therefore, to guide the intelligent and serious listener towards a deeper understanding of the masterpieces of symphony, which he is likely to hear frequently in the concert hall, over the air, or on the gramophone. (A 204)

THE CONCERTO

Edited by Ralph Hill

This is the companion volume to *The Symphony*. It follows the same plan, was completed before the editor's death in the autumn of 1950, and, though he did not live to see it through the press, it is in conception and arrangement as much his work as its companion volume.

It deals with the well-known piano, violin, and cello concertos of the present-day repertoire, and its analyses are illustrated by a wealth of musical examples. The composers whose work is considered begin with Bach, and end with William Walton; special chapters are devoted to English compositions, to the general lines of development of the concerto, and to variation forms. (A 249)

3s 6d each

JAZZ

Rex Harris

After the long and wearisome years of 'swing' which overlaid the traditions of jazz, there has arisen a new generation which is anxious to learn of the roots and growth of this fascinating folk music.

So much confusion exists in the public mind regarding the word 'jazz' that it was felt necessary to trace its ancestry and present a genealogical table which would clarify the subject.

This book is not intended to serve as a discography, or jazz directory filled with minute details of obscure gramophone records, but many examples of good jazz recordings are included, and care has been taken to select in almost every case those which are available in Great Britain at the time of writing. (A 247)

PHILHARMONIC

Thomas Russell

Philharmonic was first published in 1942 and rapidly ran into several editions. Its initial success was, perhaps, due to its double vision: that of an experienced orchestral player and of an orchestral administrator. Some of the ideas put forward showed considerable originality, but were soon accepted and acted upon by the author's colleagues. The realization of these ideas has led to the re-writing of several chapters, for Thomas Russell does not believe that the social development of music can be allowed to stand still.

A faith in the capacity of the man-in-the-street to appreciate the best in music, and an abhorrence of cliques, give to this book a sane optimism which is as good a tonic to-day as when it first appeared. A 264)

2s each

GOING TO THE BALLET

Arnold Haskell

Who thinks up a ballet? How does he combine the work of the different artists involved? Which are the best ballets? Is there more than one kind of dancing? These are some of the questions answered in this book, which has 32 pages of plates. (PS 86)

ENJOYING PAINTINGS

A. C. Ward

A book to help children look at pictures, illustrated with many photographs of famous paintings. (PS 84)

GOING TO A CONCERT

Lionel Salter

Explains how the orchestra is made up, the importance of each instrument, how a composer sets about his work, how to read a score, and many other things to help children to listen to music. It has many photographs of musicians and the orchestra. (PS 85)

2s 6d each